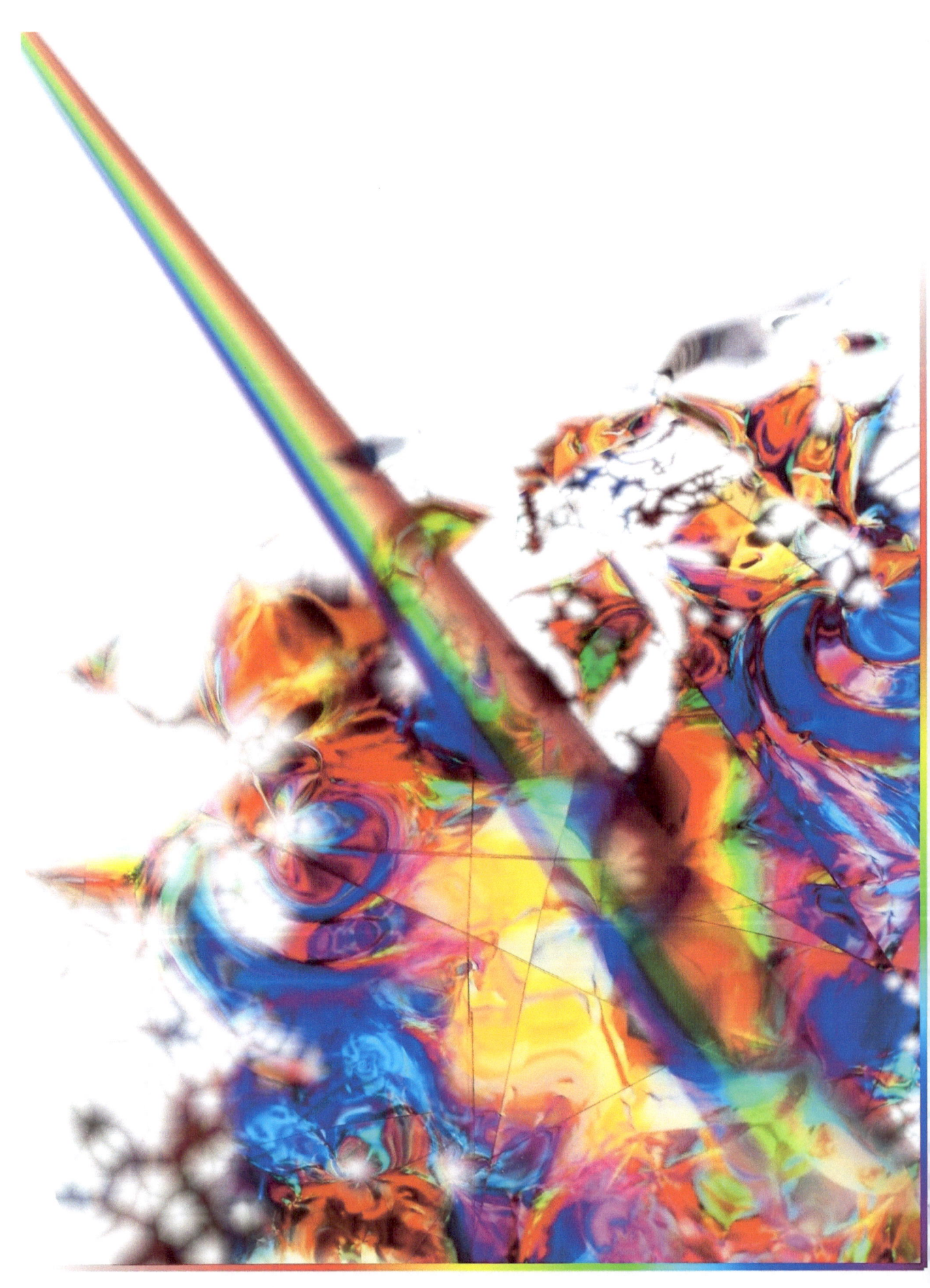

Artisan of Light: 2015

A unique abstract art form

Robert B. Calkins

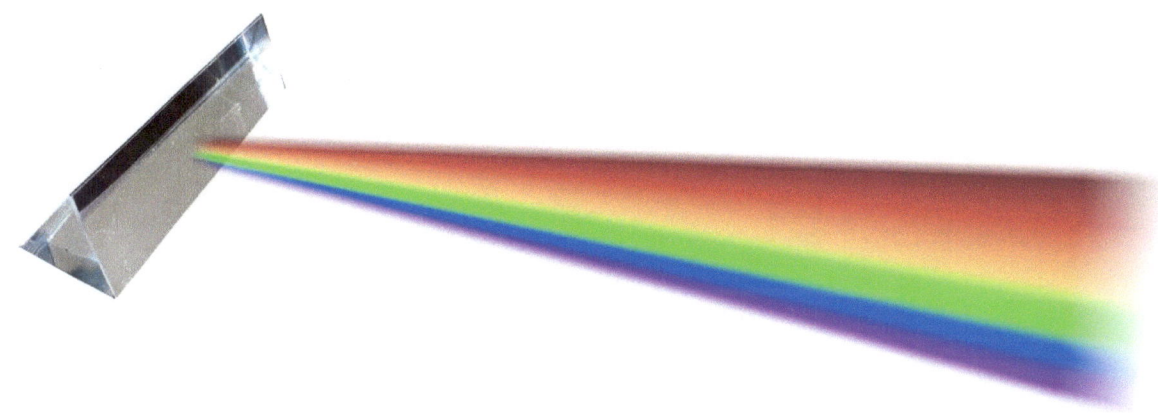

Published by Robert B. Calkins
Issaquah, WA

Printed by CreateSpace

Calkins, Robert B.
  Art, Abstract, Sunlight, Art form, Integral.

ISBN-13: 978-1523938421

Edition 1.0

https://www.amazon.com/author/robertbcalkins

Cover art and design by Robert B. Calkins

Artisan of Light   My award winning art begins with sun light, the source of energy that powers all life on earth. It represents the vitality and exuberance of life itself. My work/play attempts to capture that exuberance and its variety.

My palette is an array of glass prisms which creates the rich colors of the rainbow. Adjusting the individual prisms makes additional color combinations beyond the normal rainbow of a single prism. Using lens, filters, reflections, foam board, glue, paint, overhead transparencies and other objects I create various light effects and take digital photographs of the results. The final process involves using a computer to manipulate the images (such as crop, cut, paste, etc.). I classify my art as mostly non-representational abstract mixed media.

My process and tools were developed over a number of years of experimentation, a sample of which is shown in below.

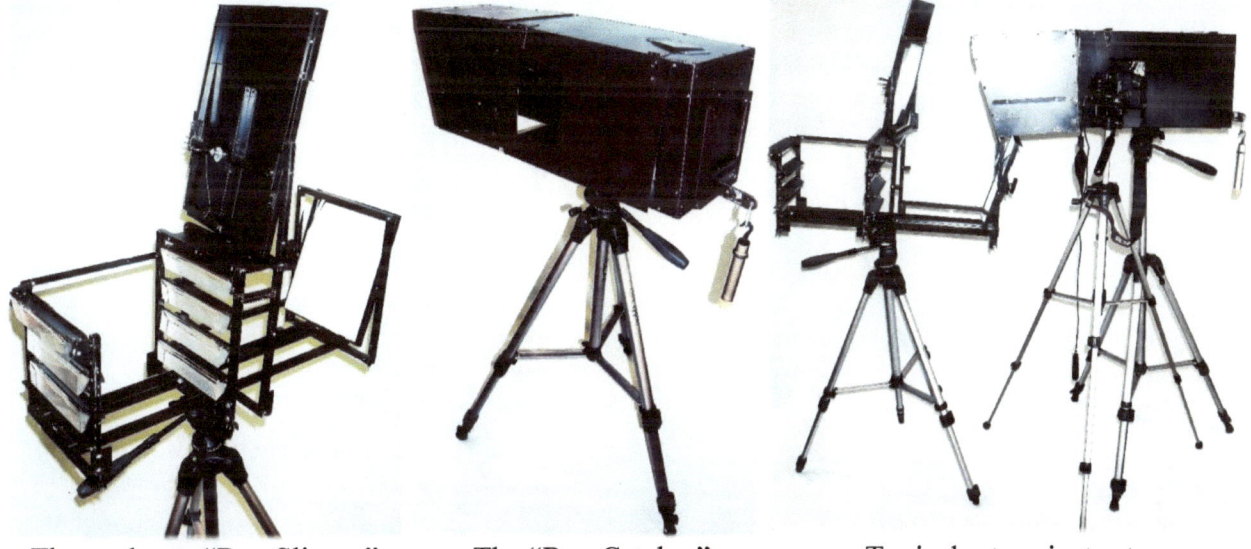

| The sunbeam "Ray Slinger" | The "Ray Catcher" | Typical art project set up |

One irony of this art form is that it starts with sun light and I not only live in the Pacific Northwest but in heavily forested woods. The only time of the year I can get appropriate sun in my studio is on sunny mornings between 9 am and 11 am, late May through August. My response to this obstacle has been to make my studio mobile. When the sun is shining but not in my studio, I take my show on the road to find a sunny spot to set up the portable studio. One favorite spot is the top floor of park-and-ride garages (photo below).

In addition to my art, I am interested in integral philosophy and have authored a book. I have two bachelors and two master's degrees and am retired from a career in aerospace R&D.

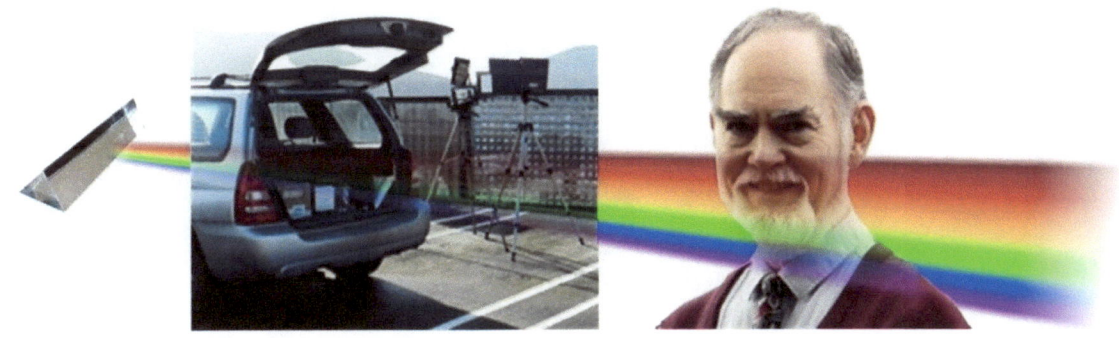

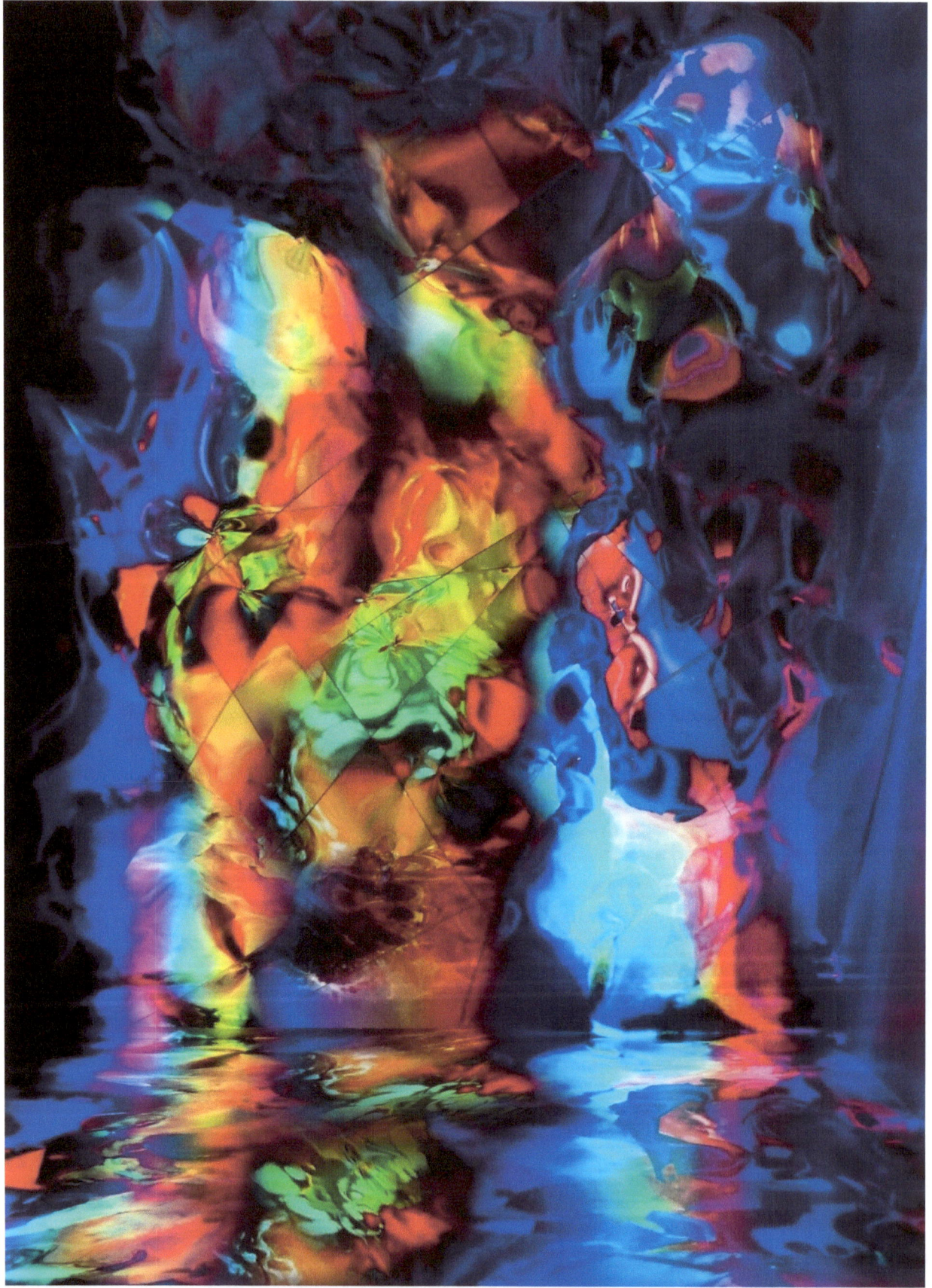

Unsupported Assumptions

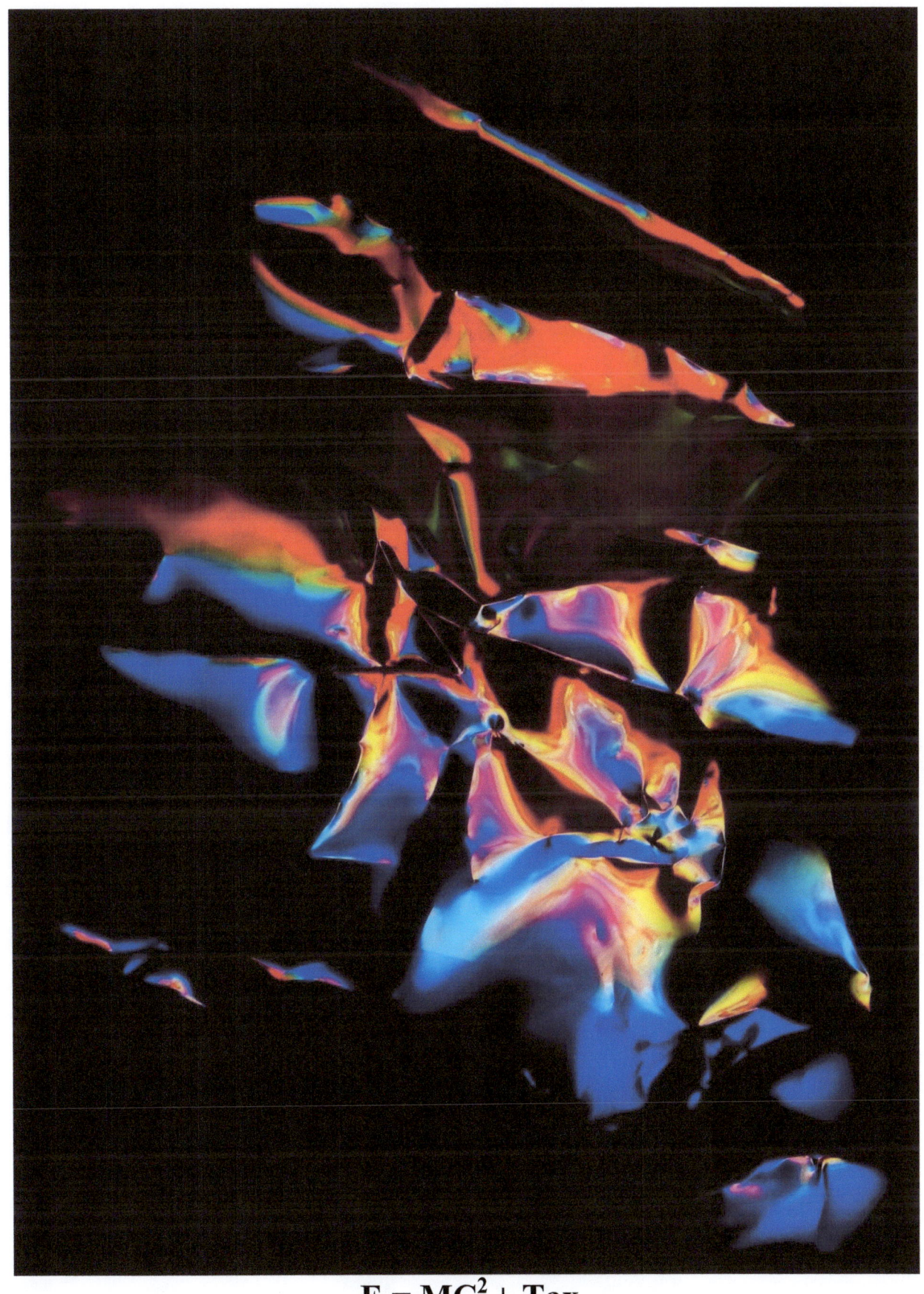

$$E = MC^2 + Tax$$

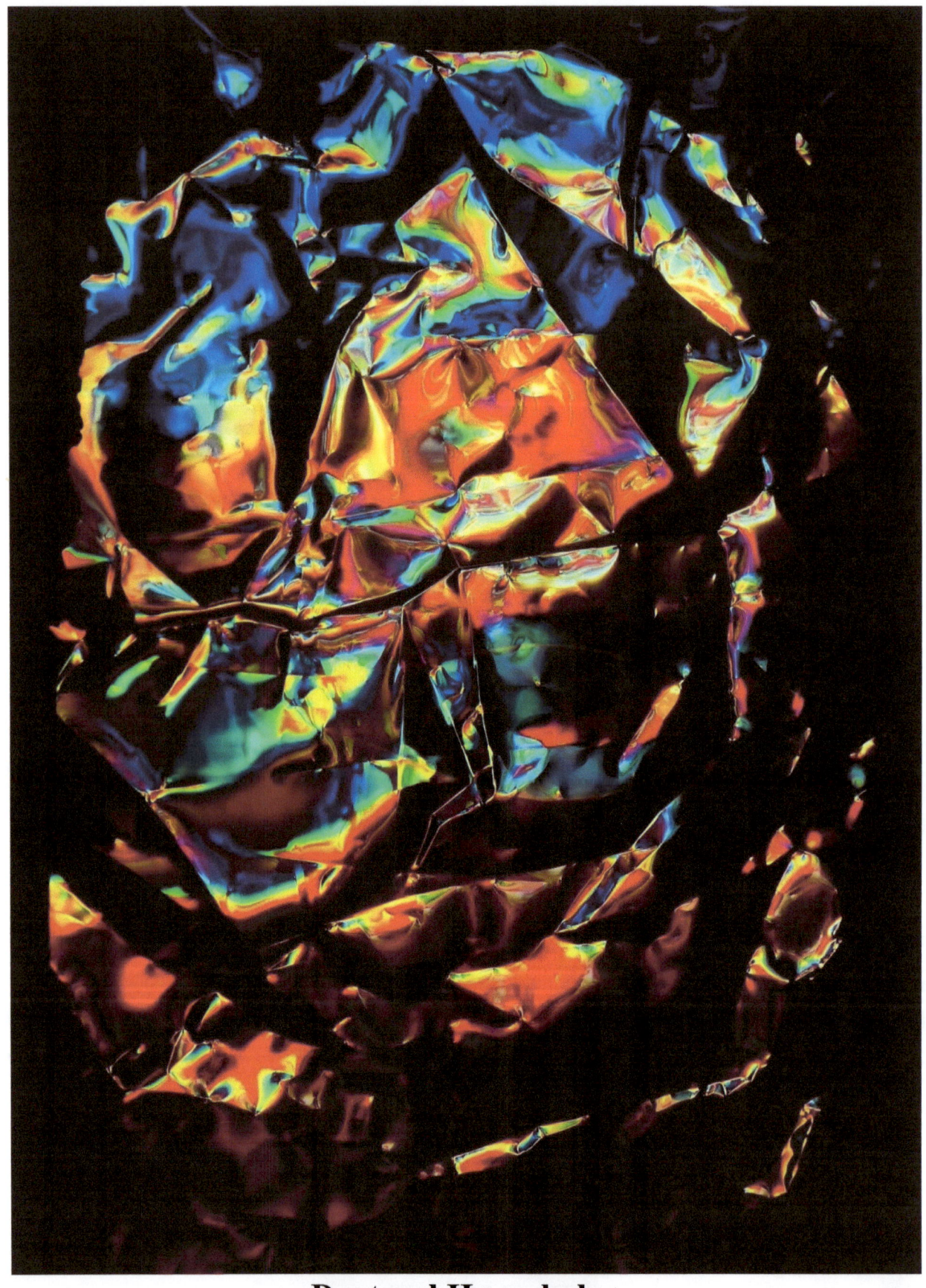

Doctoral Hyperbolae

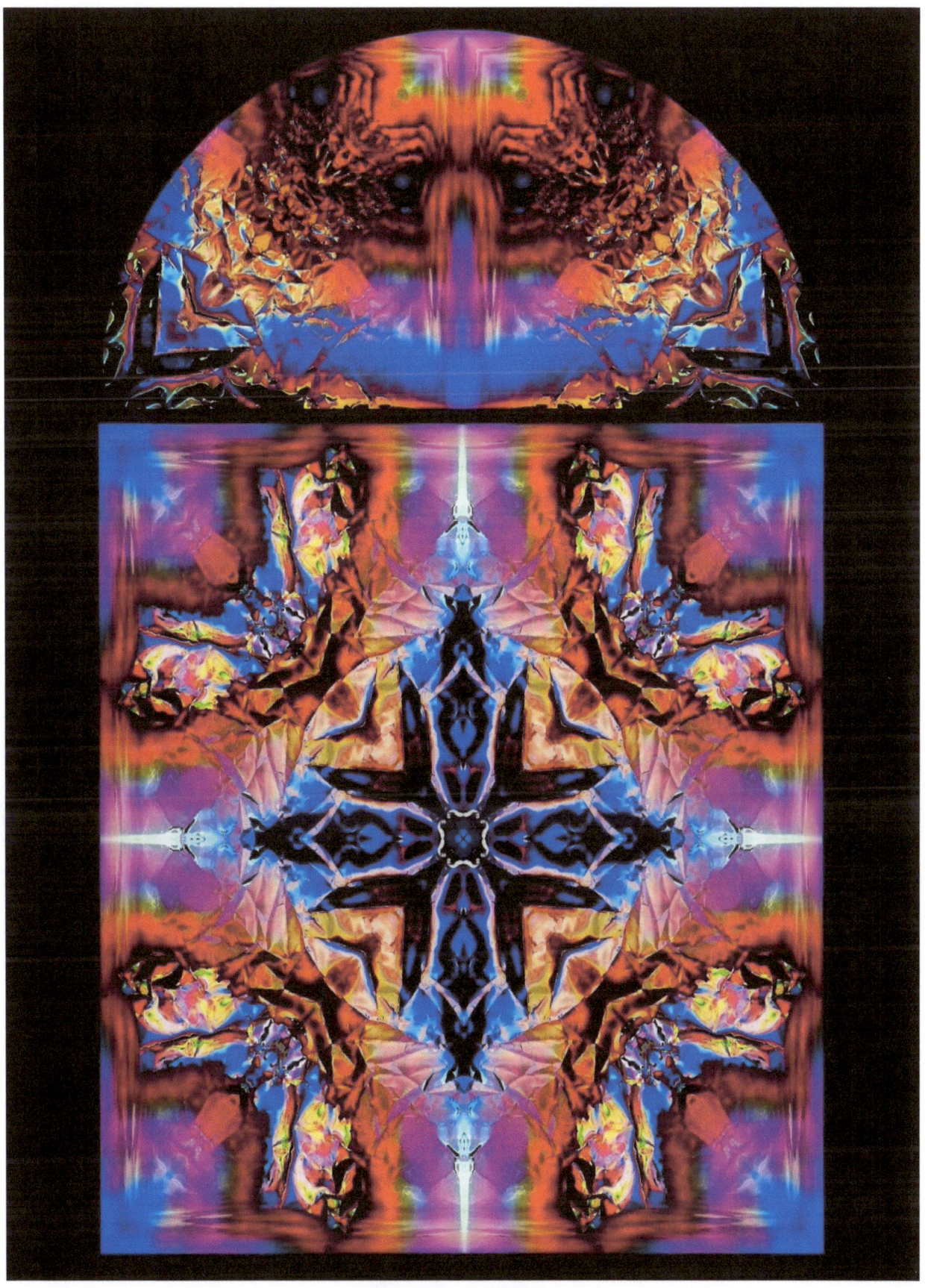

Stained Glass

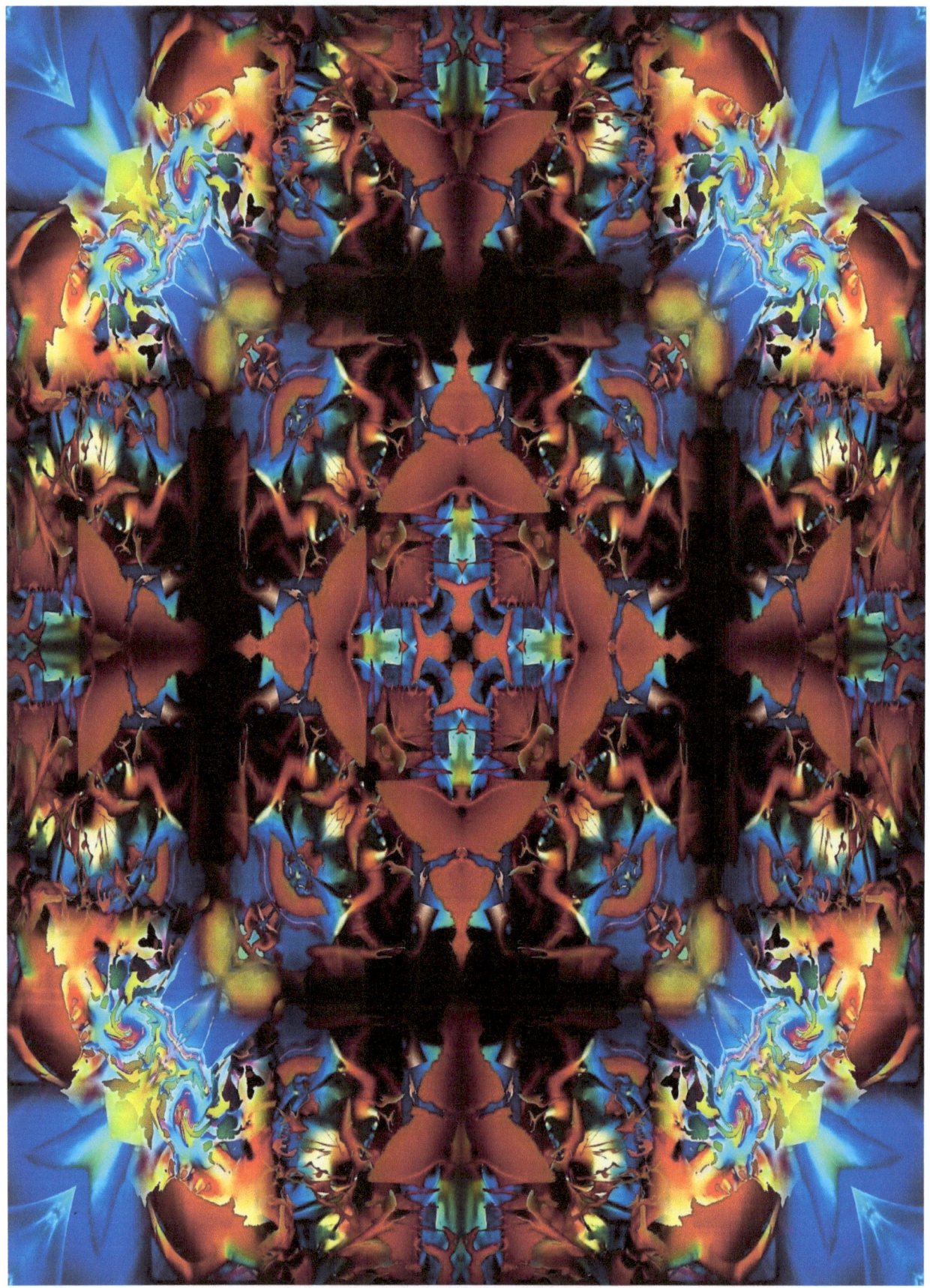

Social Obligation

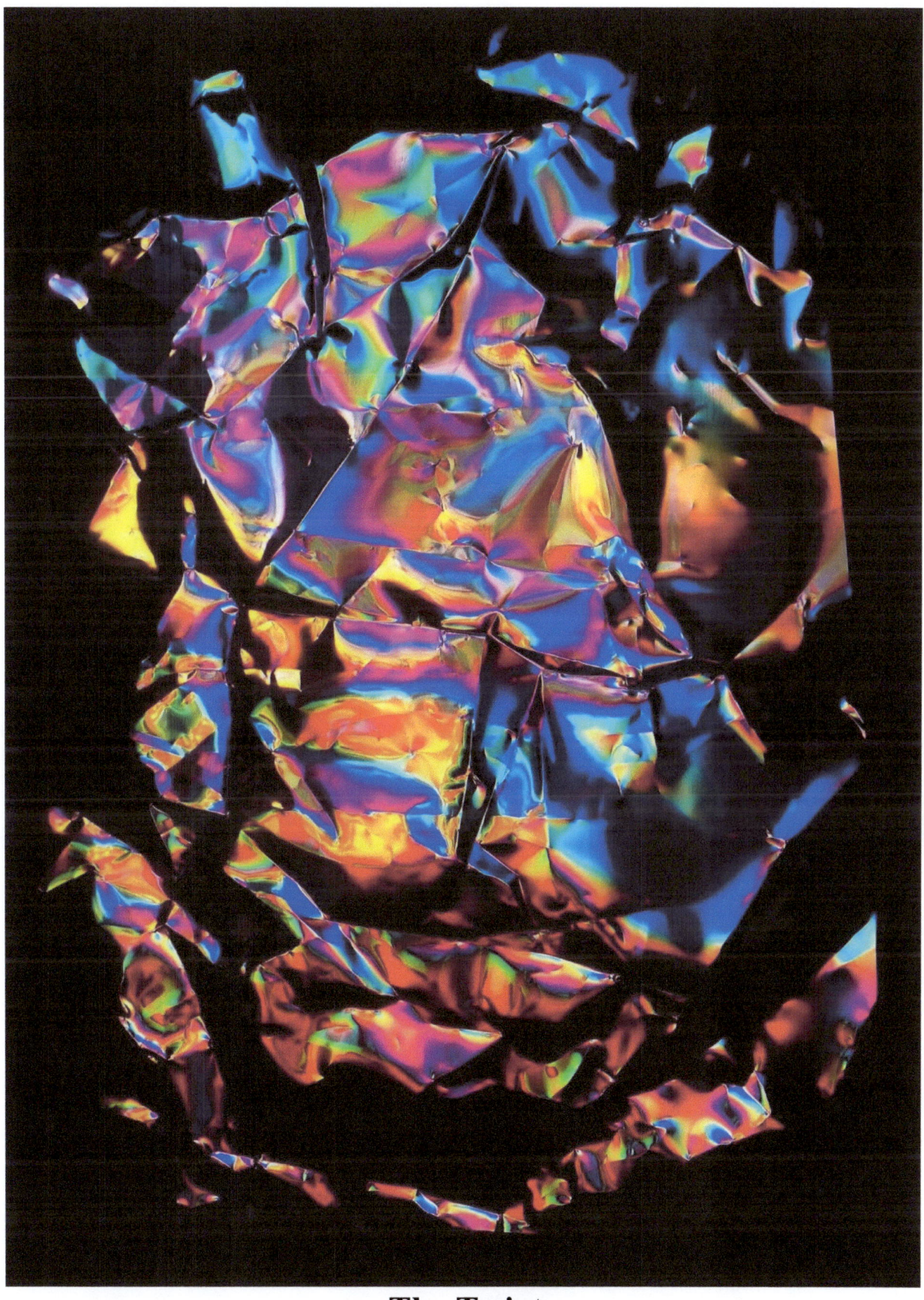

The Twixt

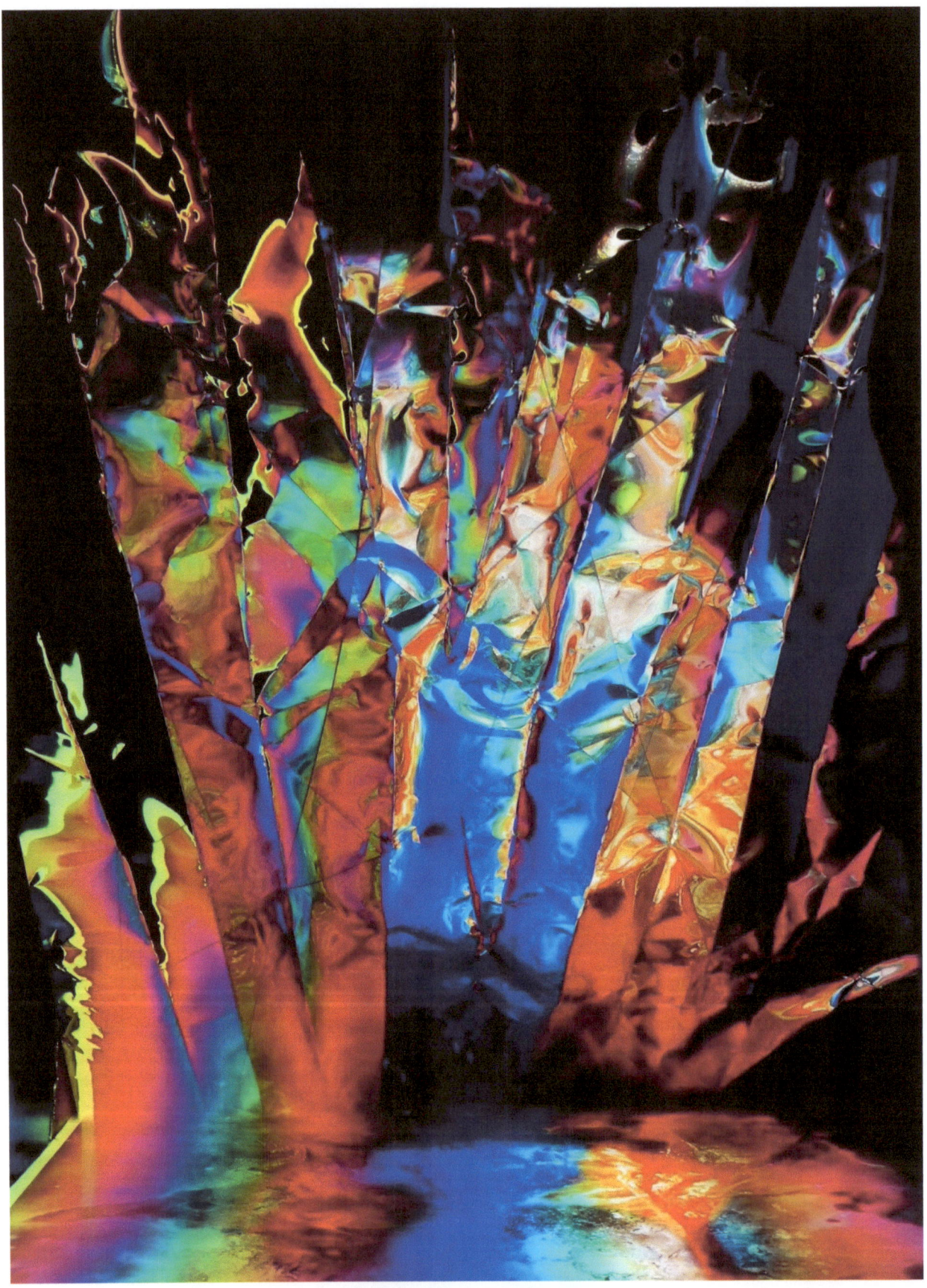

Sonic Boomslang

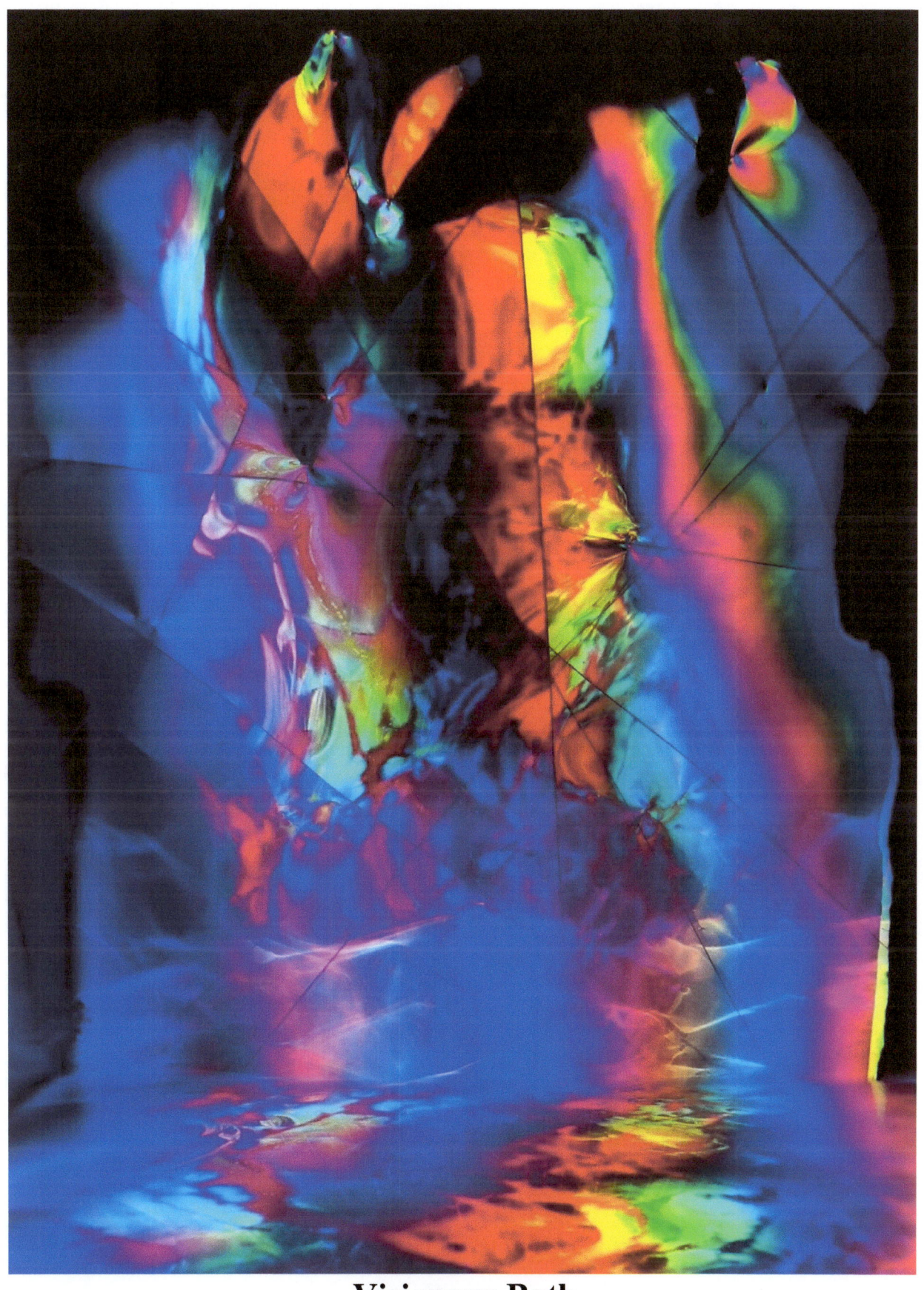

Visionary Bath

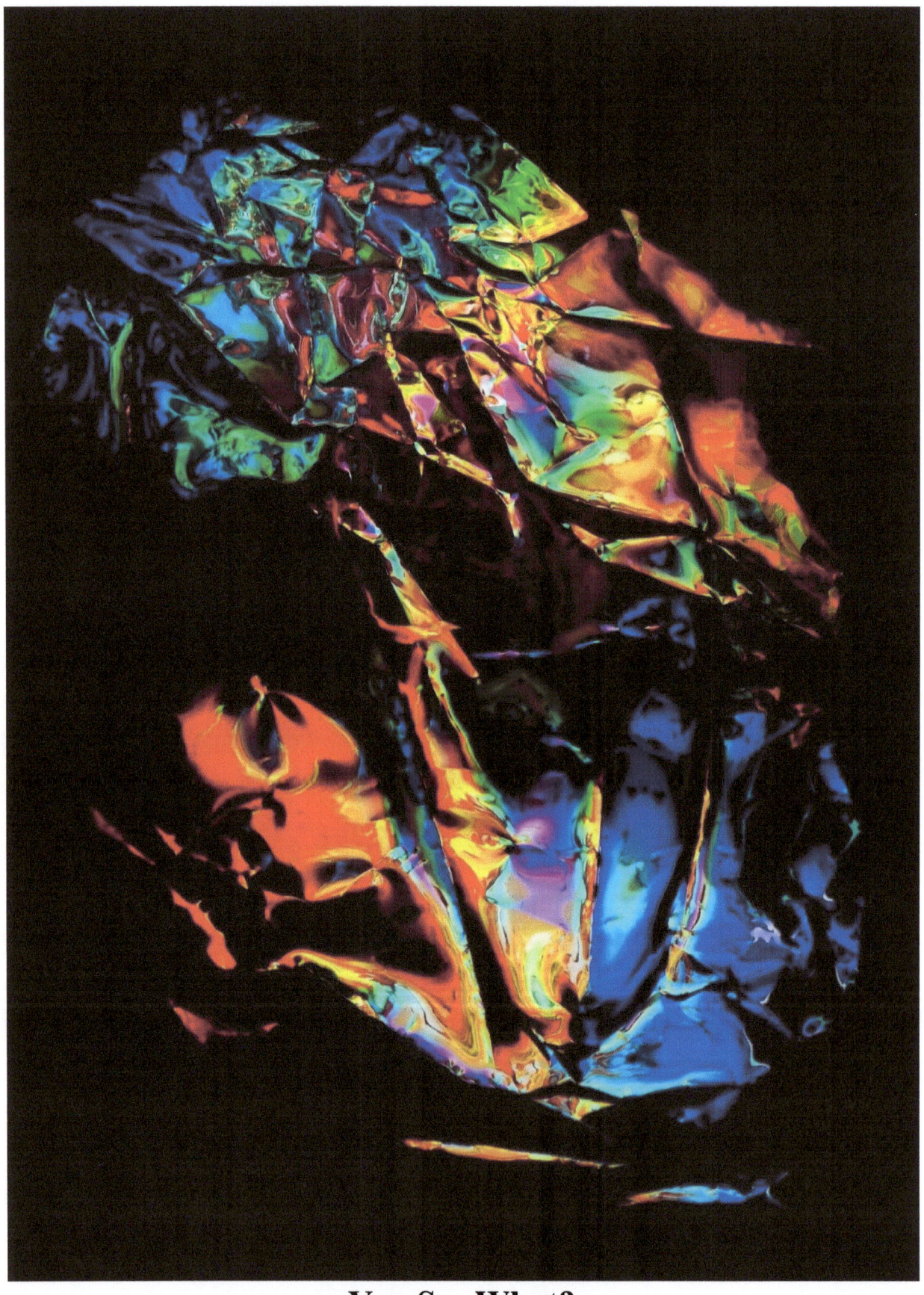

You See What?

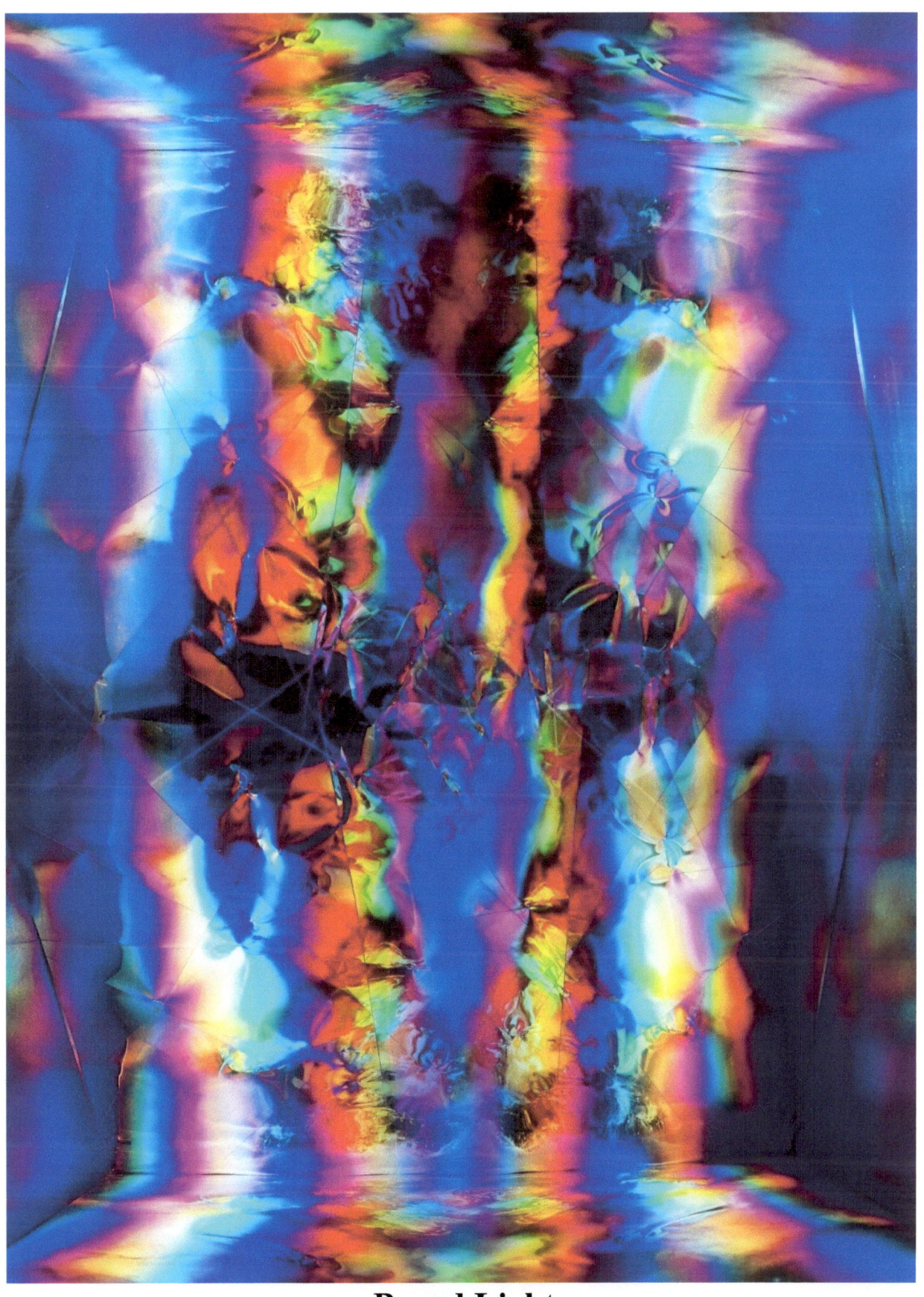

Boxed Light

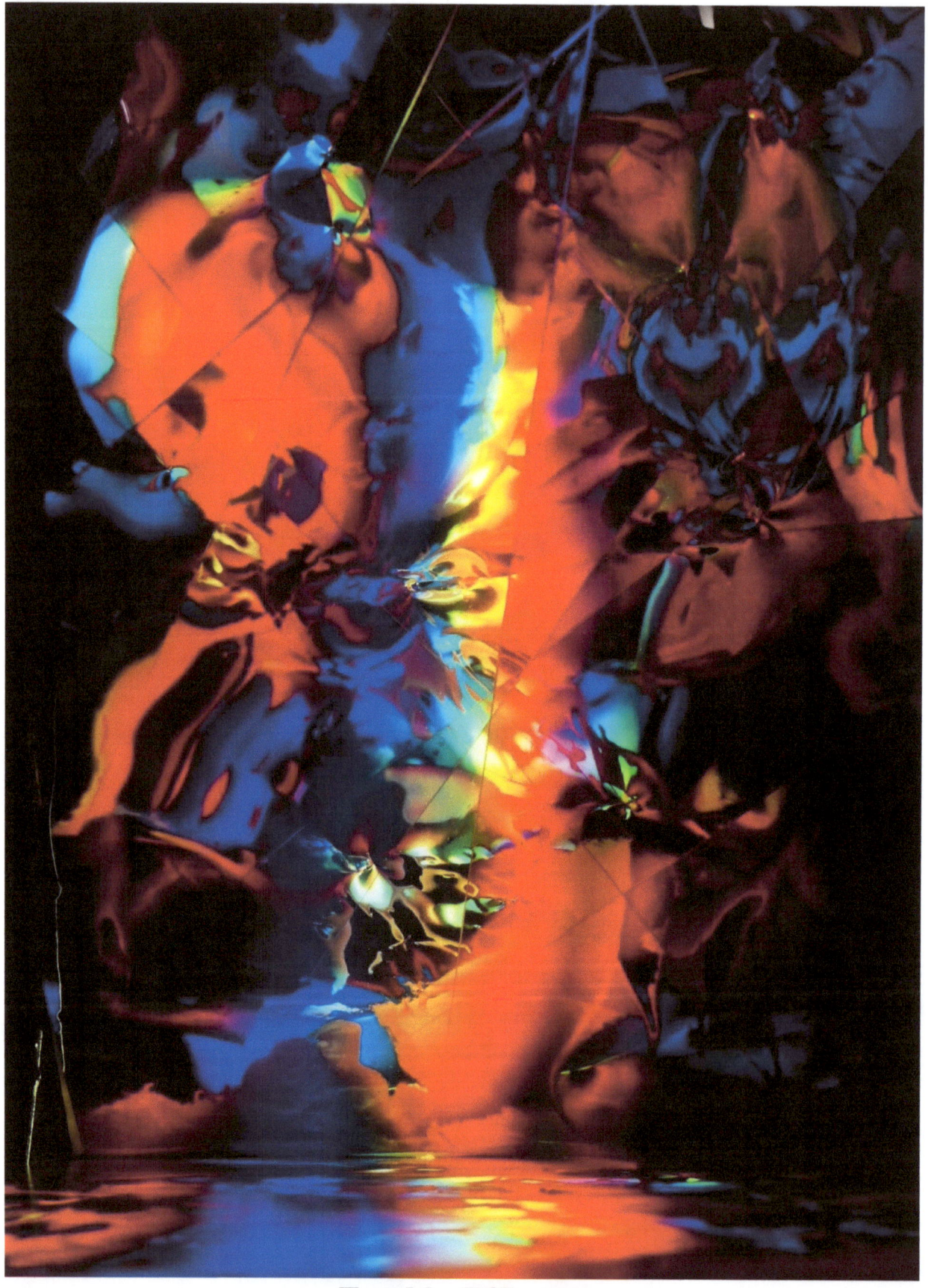

Earthly Effluent

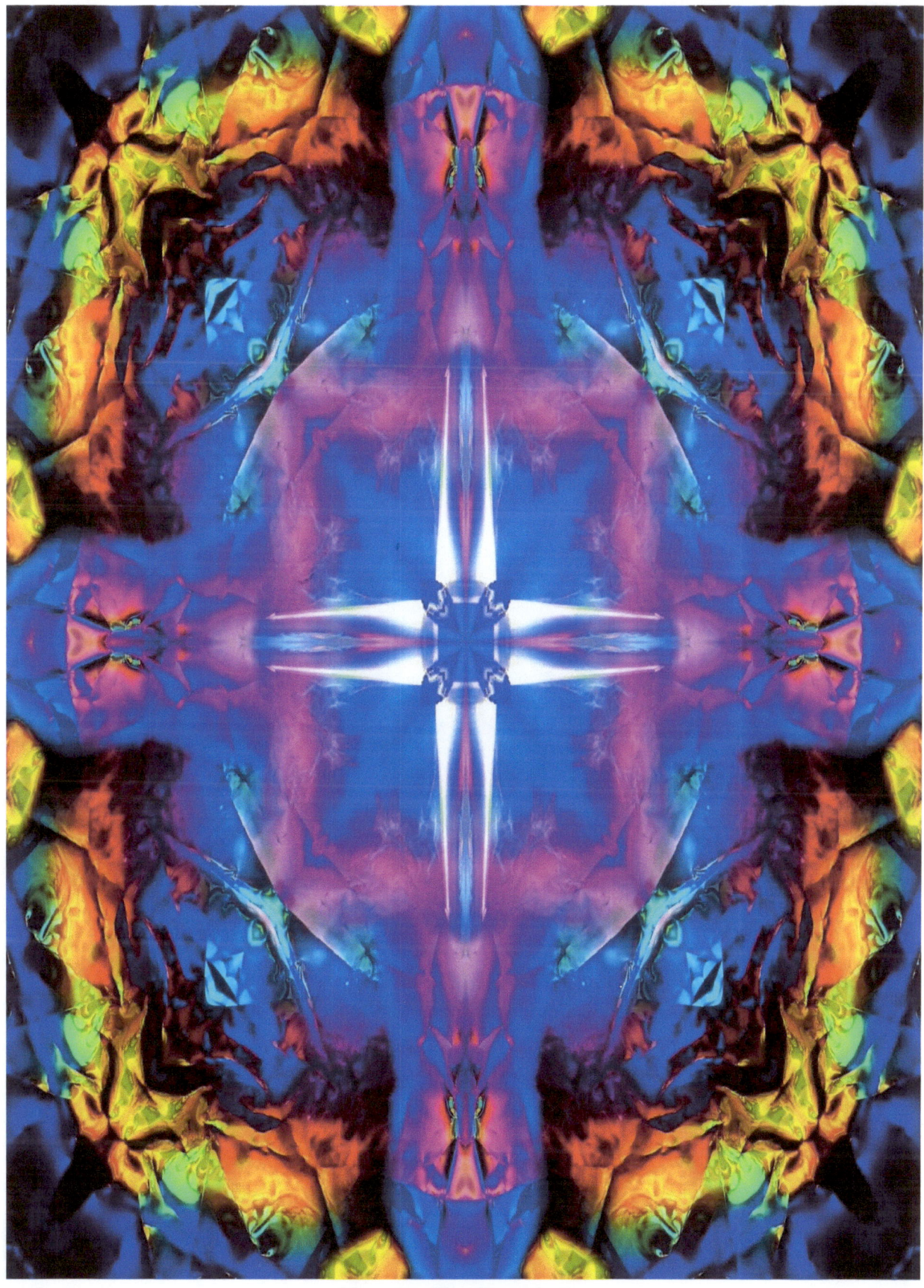

Egoic Reflections

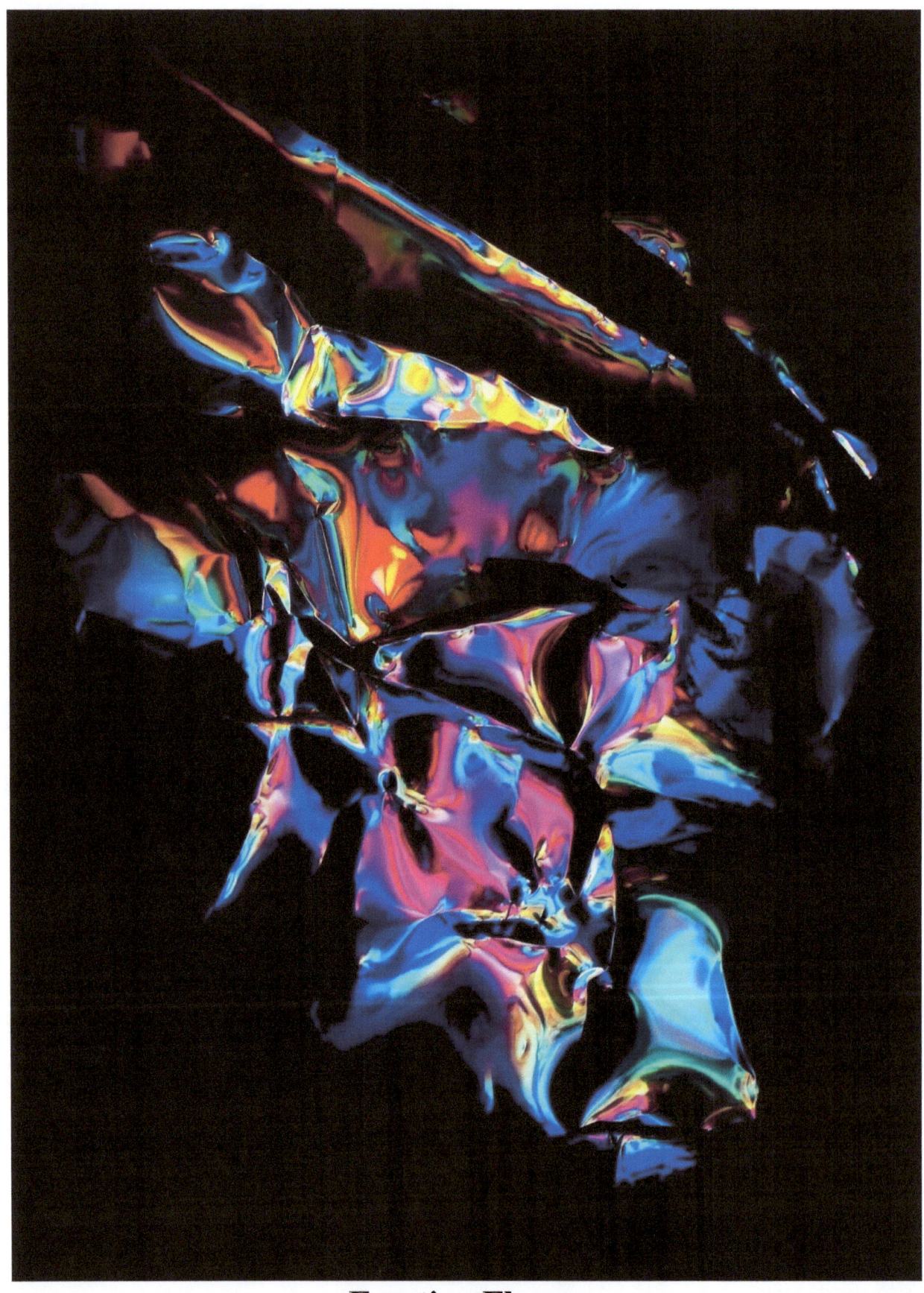

Emotion Flurry

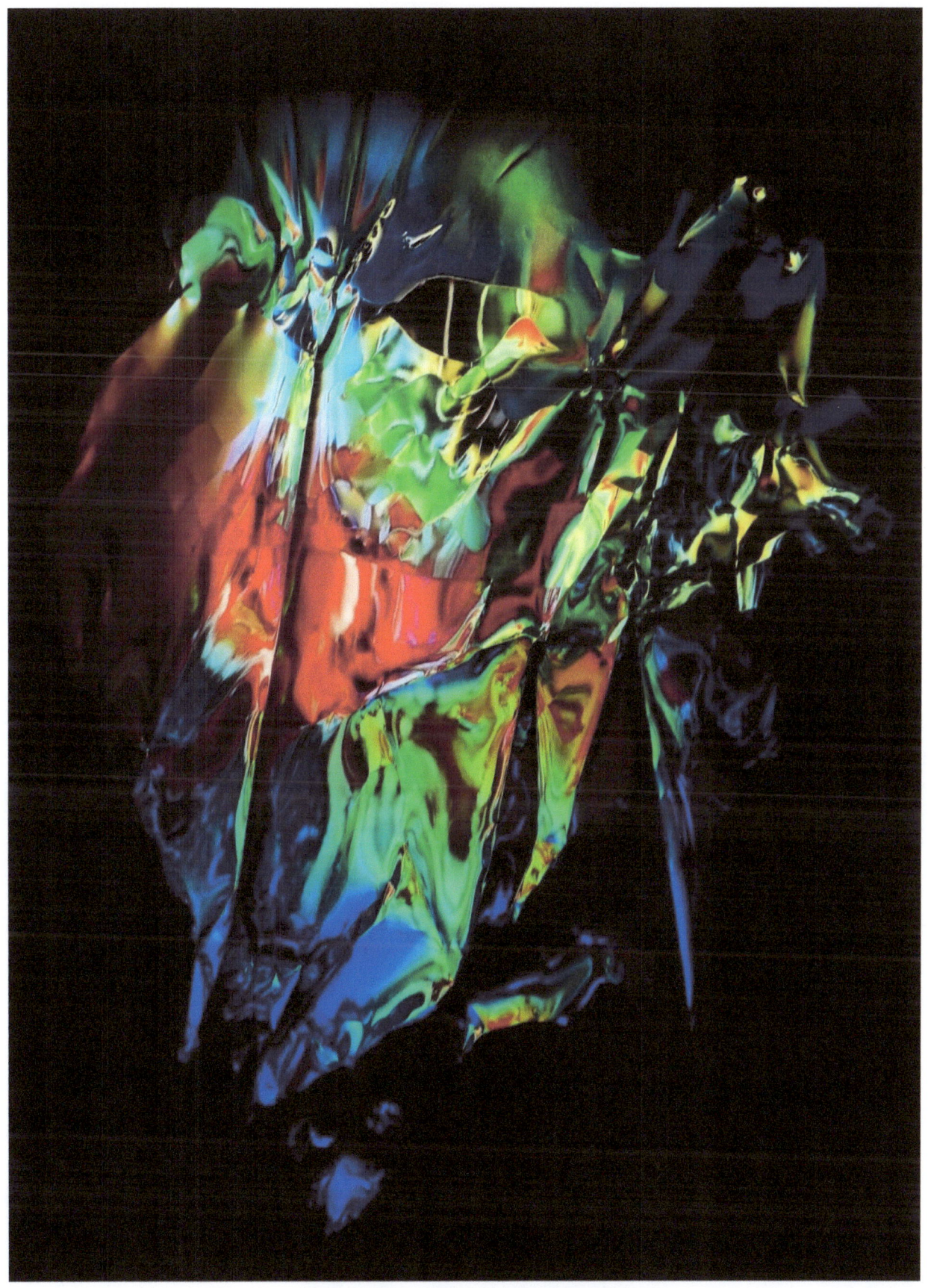

Mental Chewing Gum

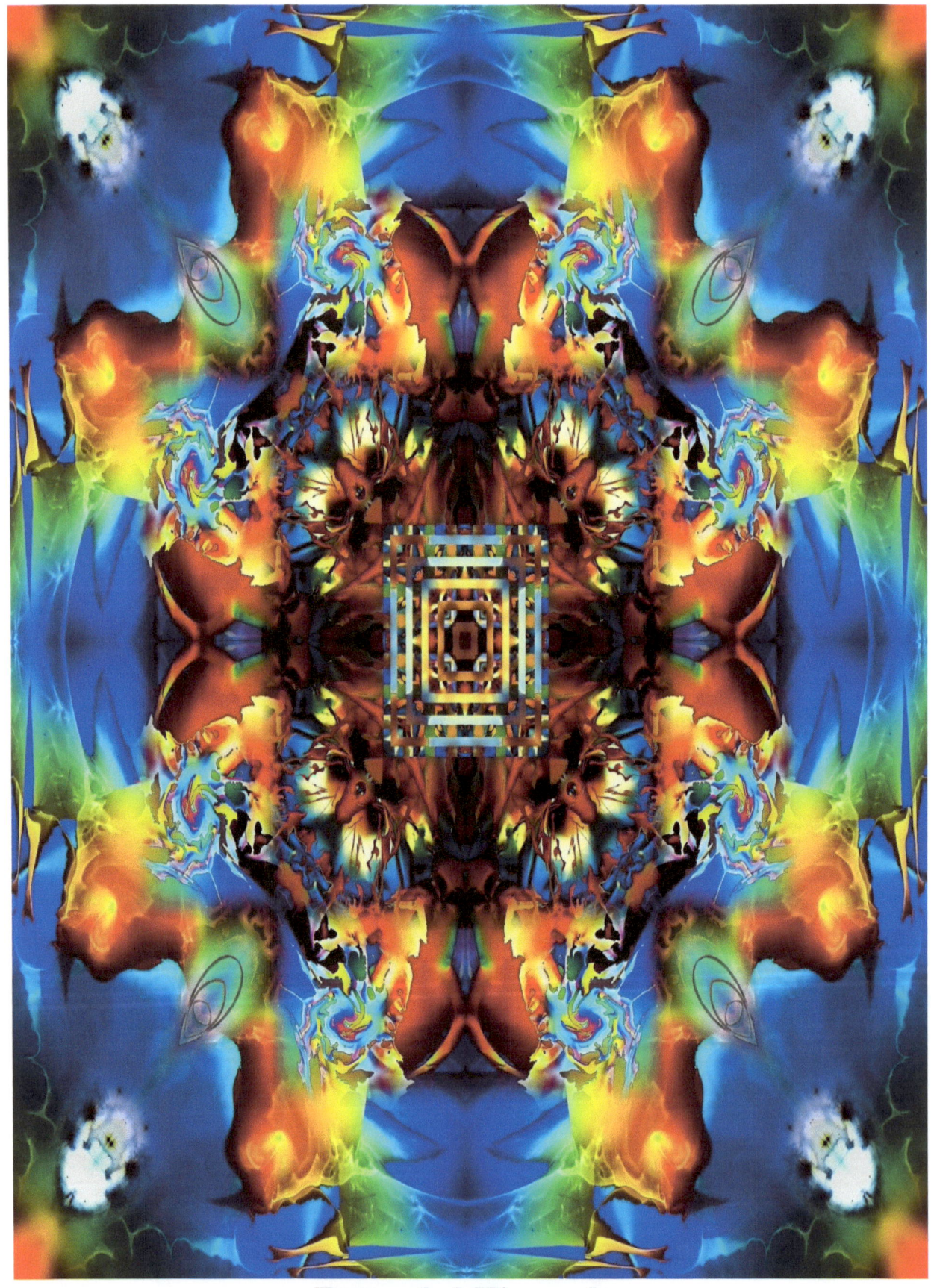

Entangled Hierarchy

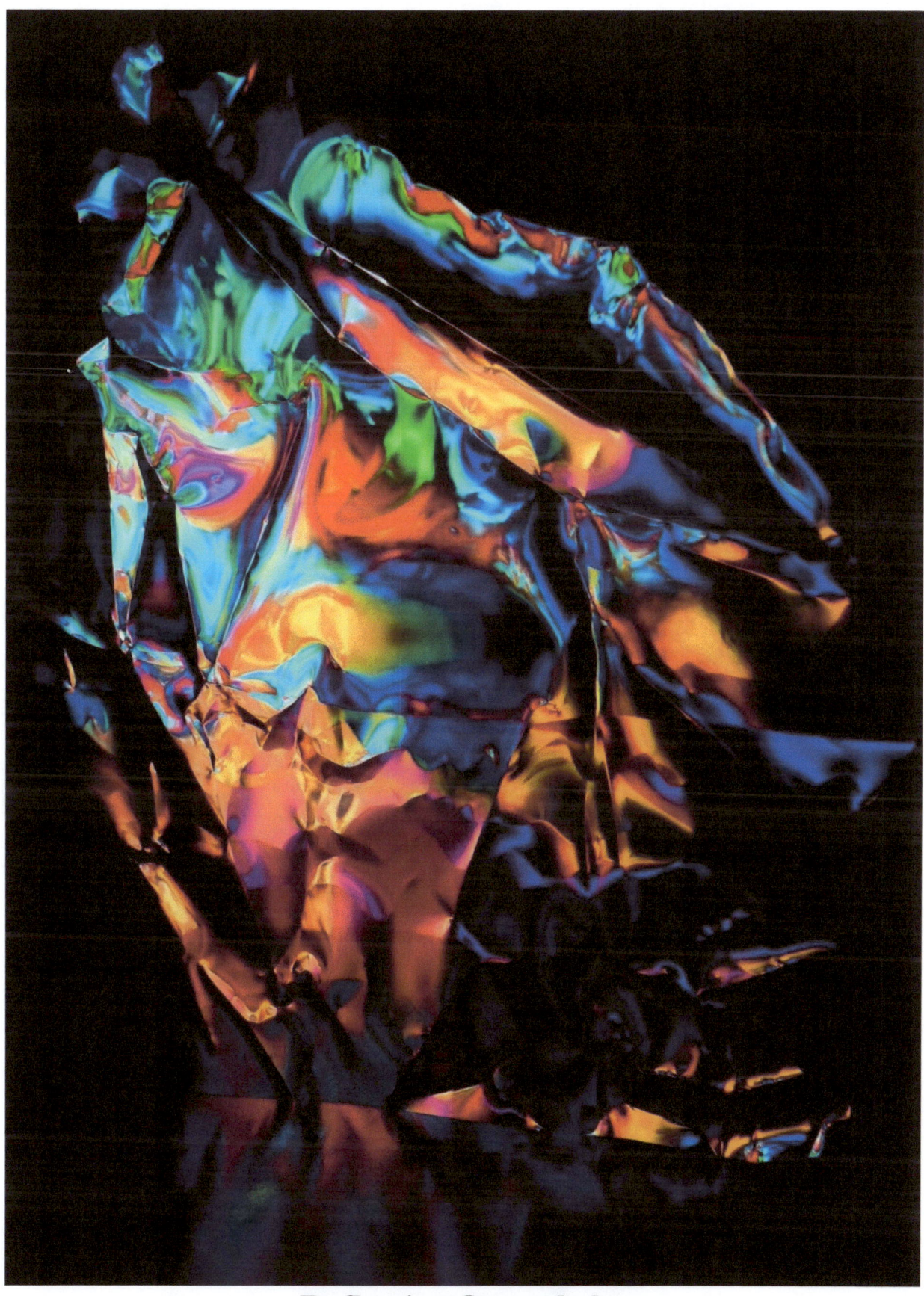

Reflective Overwhelm

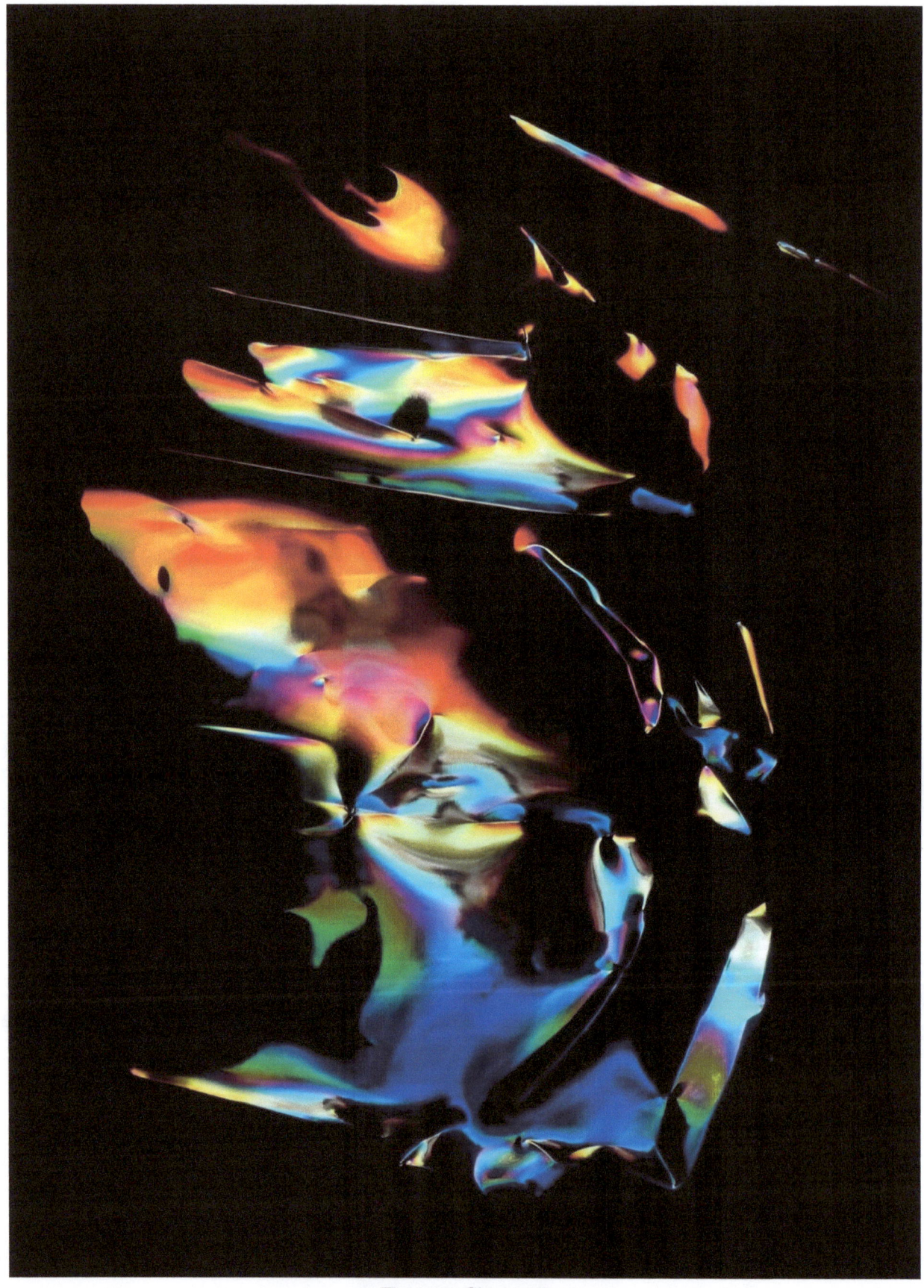

Root Canal

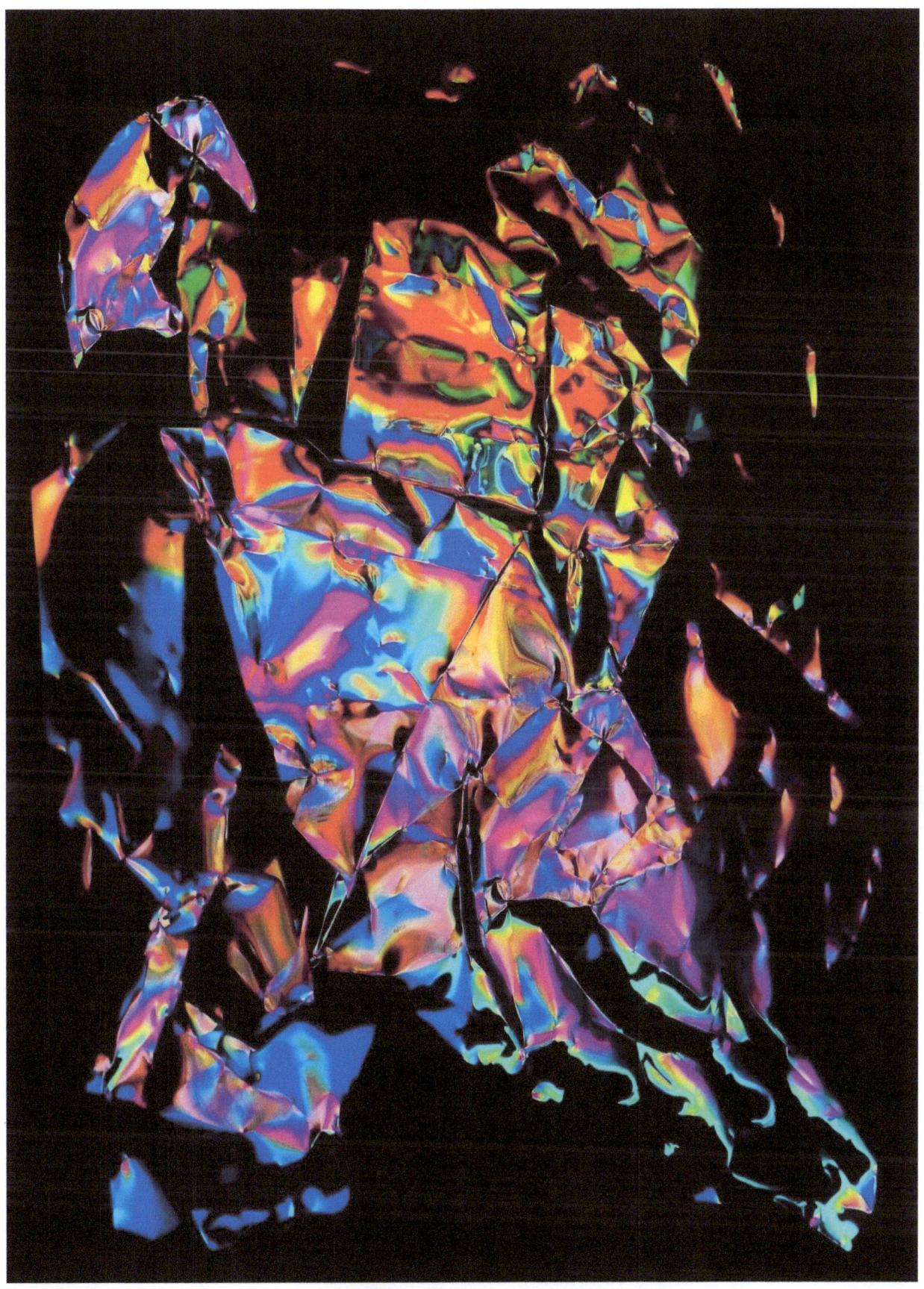

Slight Workaround

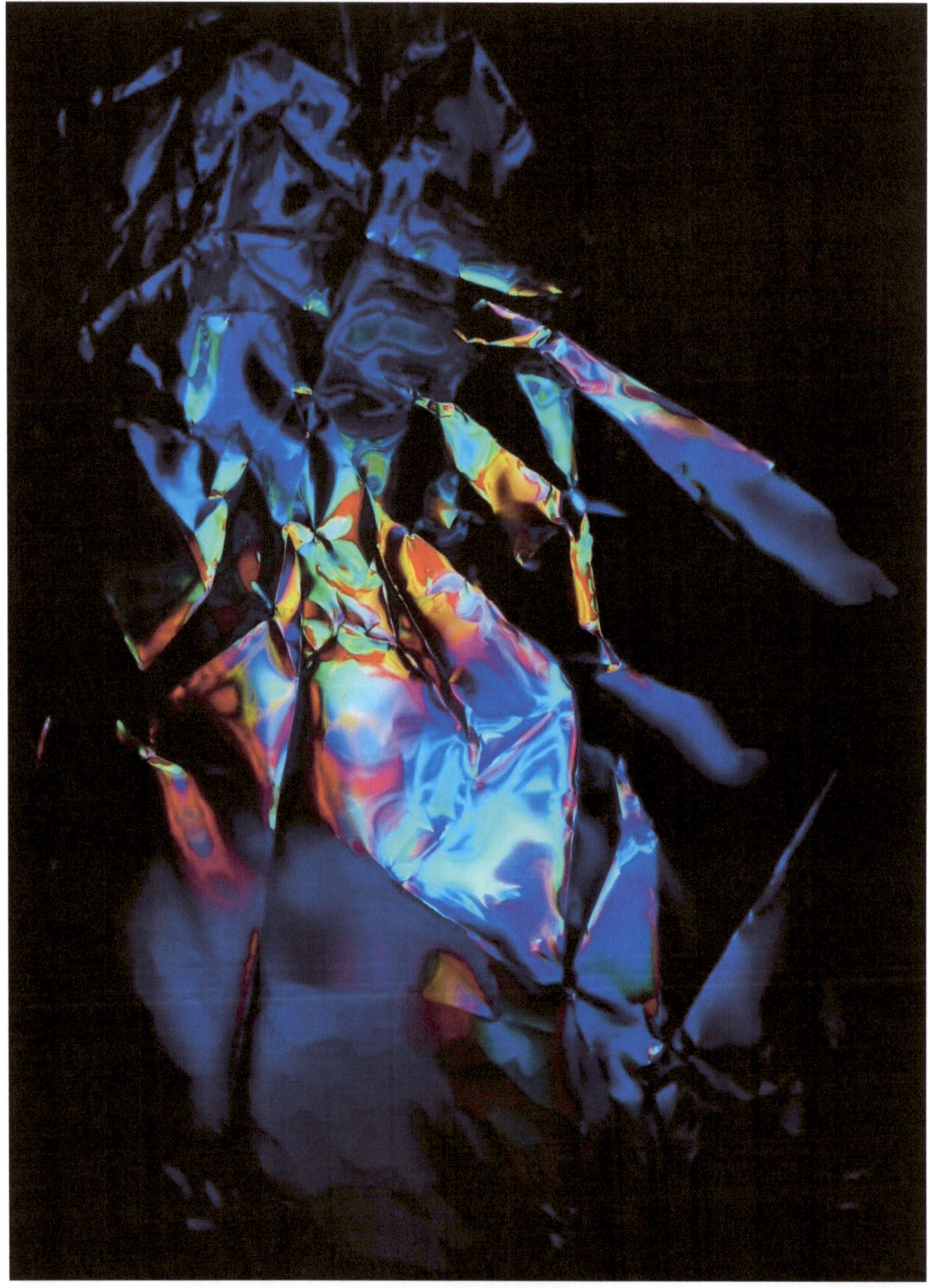

Blue Girl

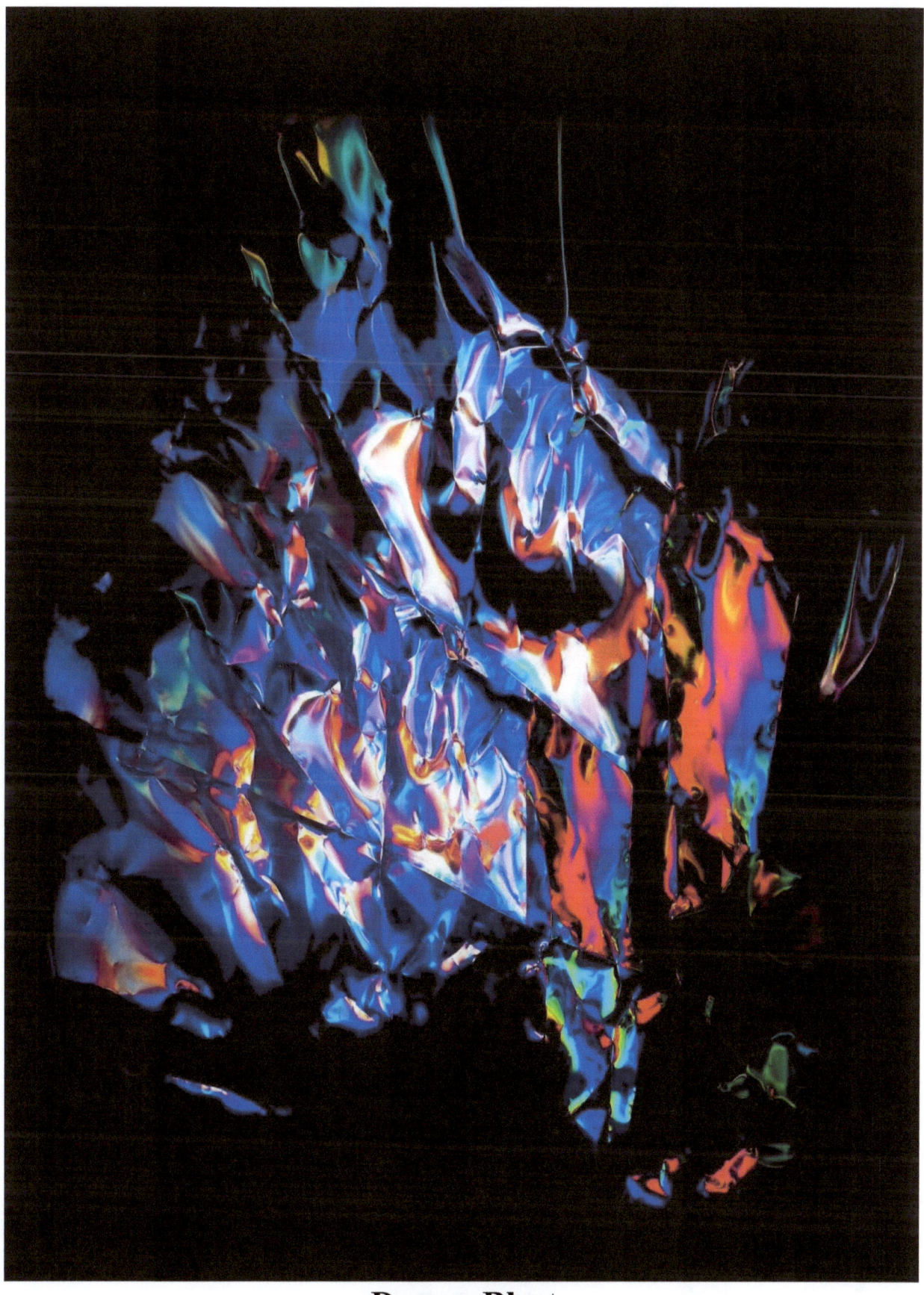

Dream Blast

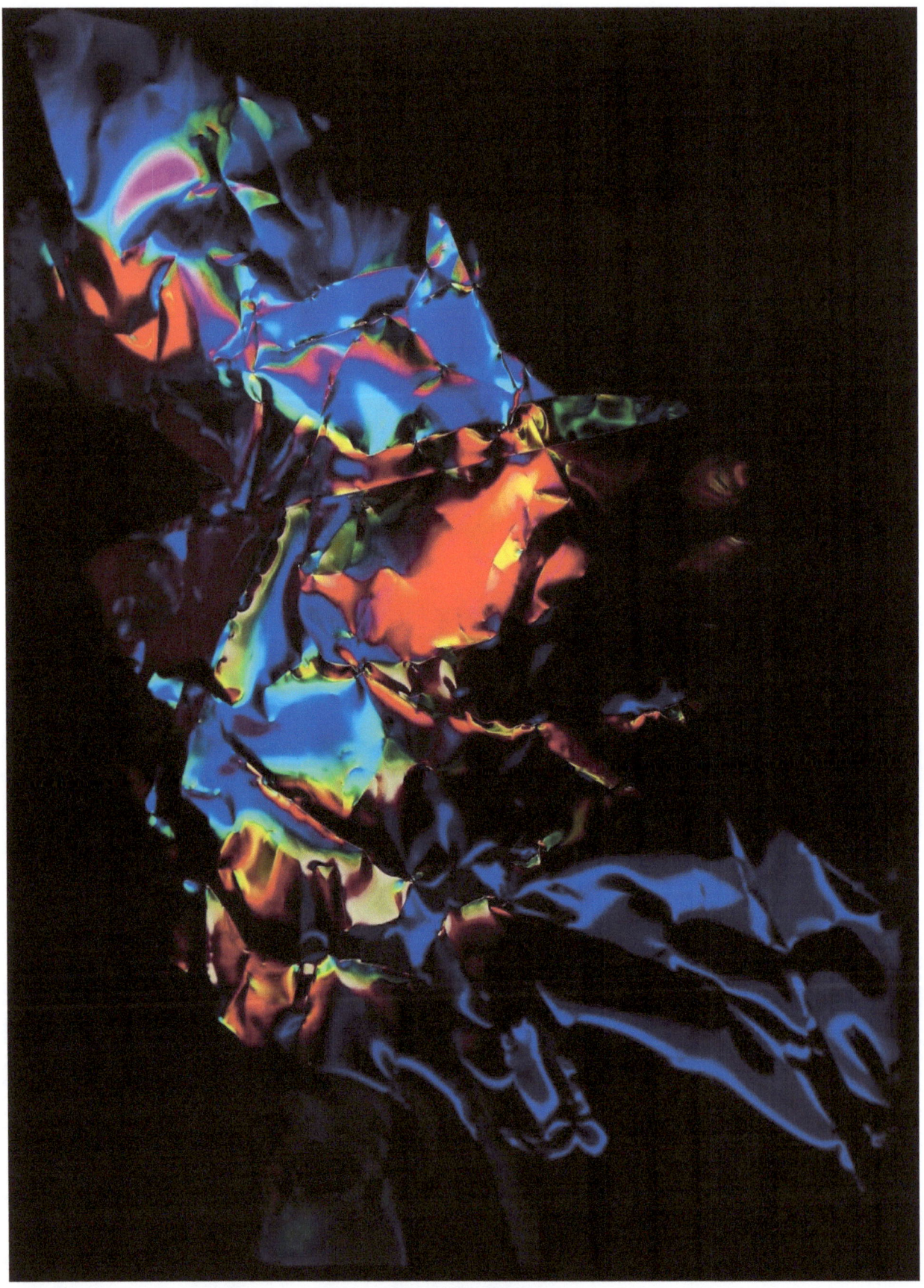

Can It Be?

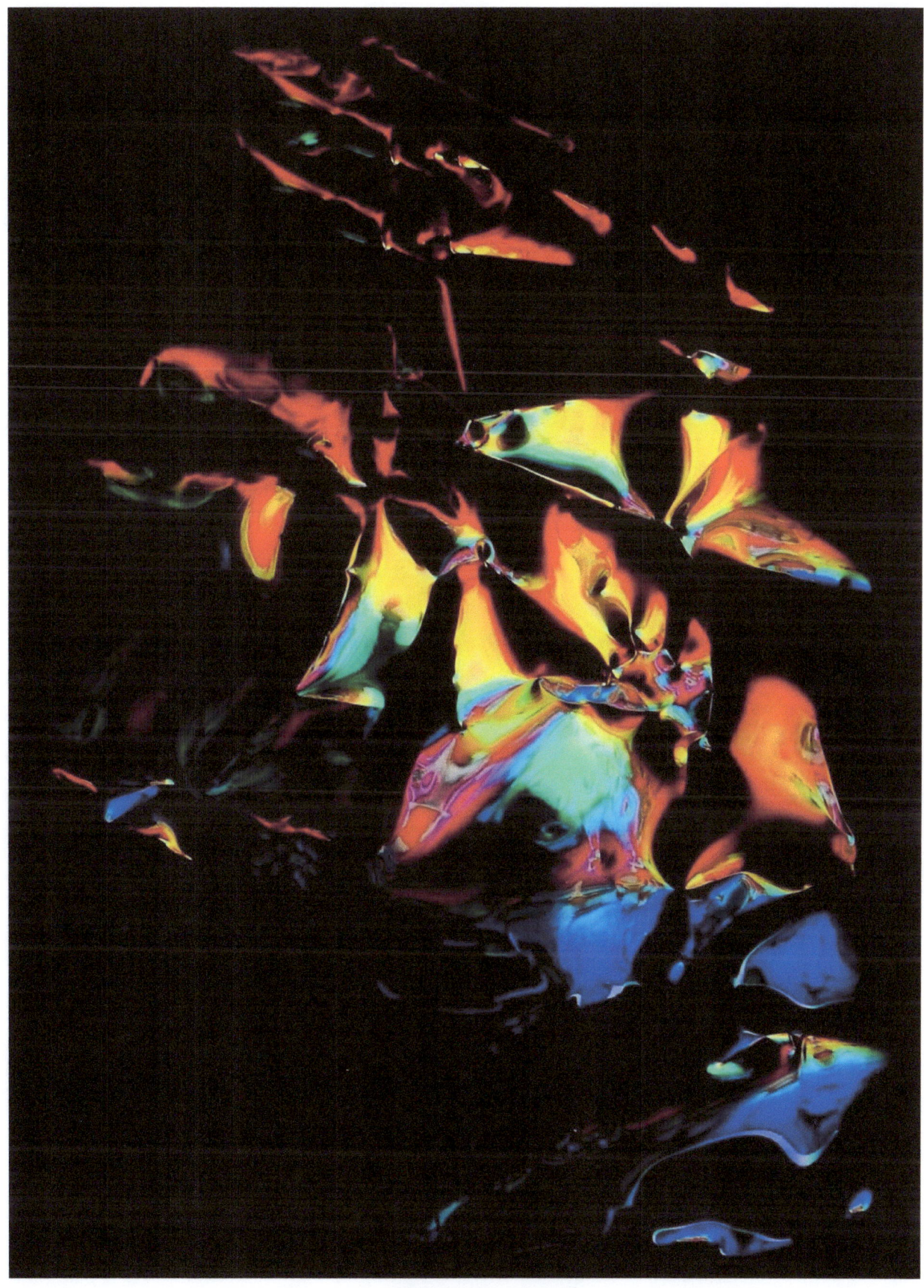

This Is It

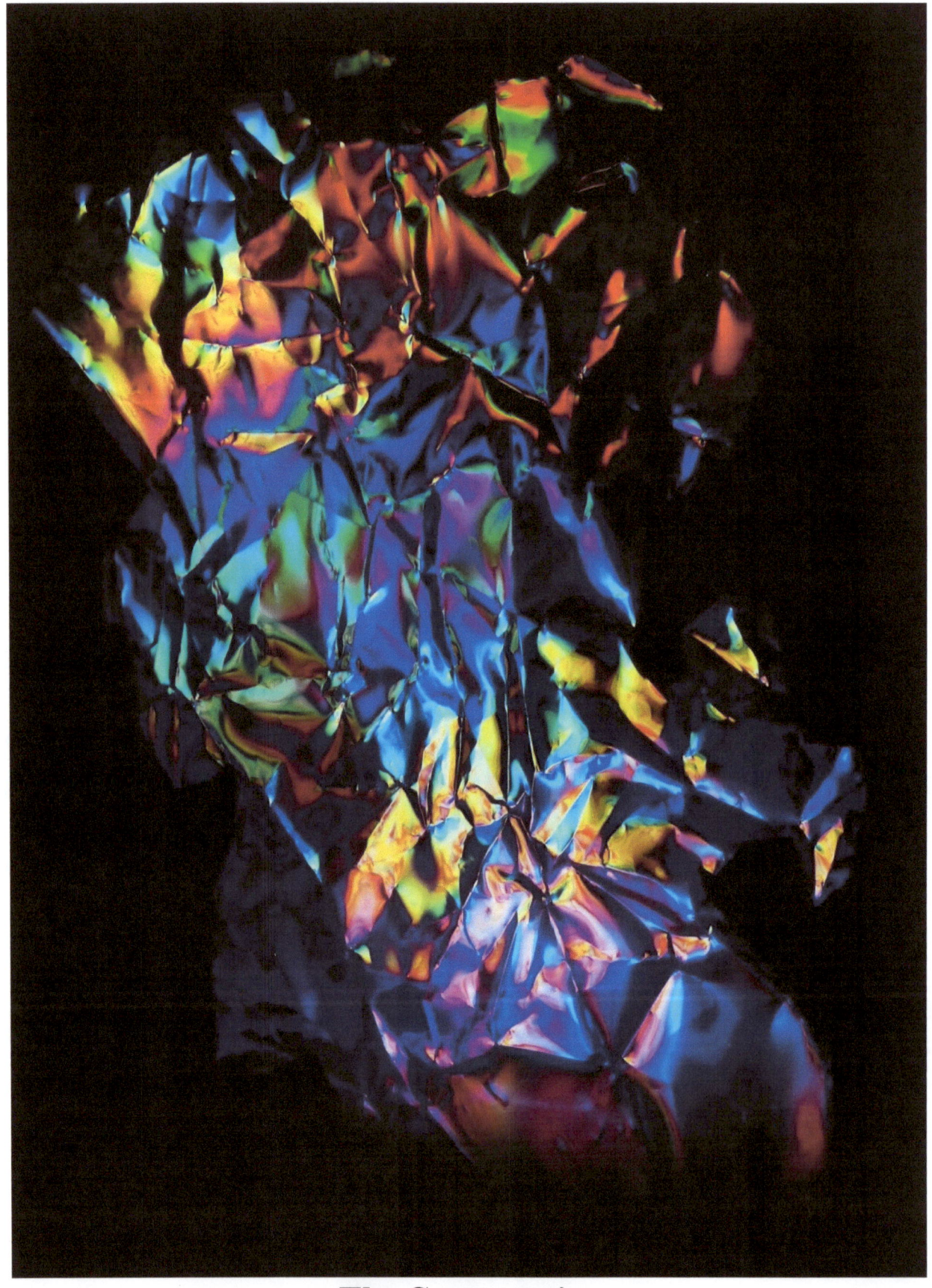

The Compromise

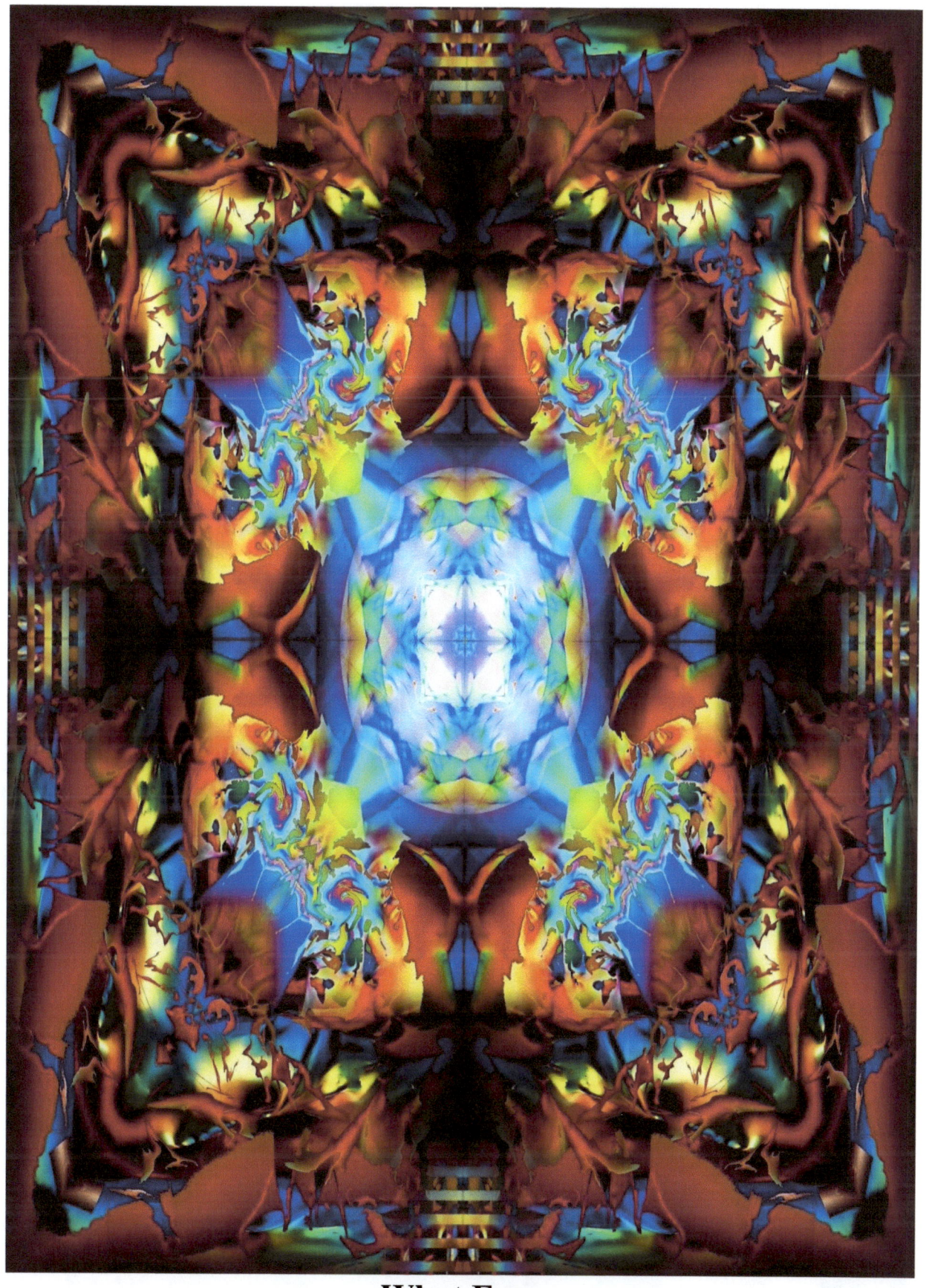

What Four

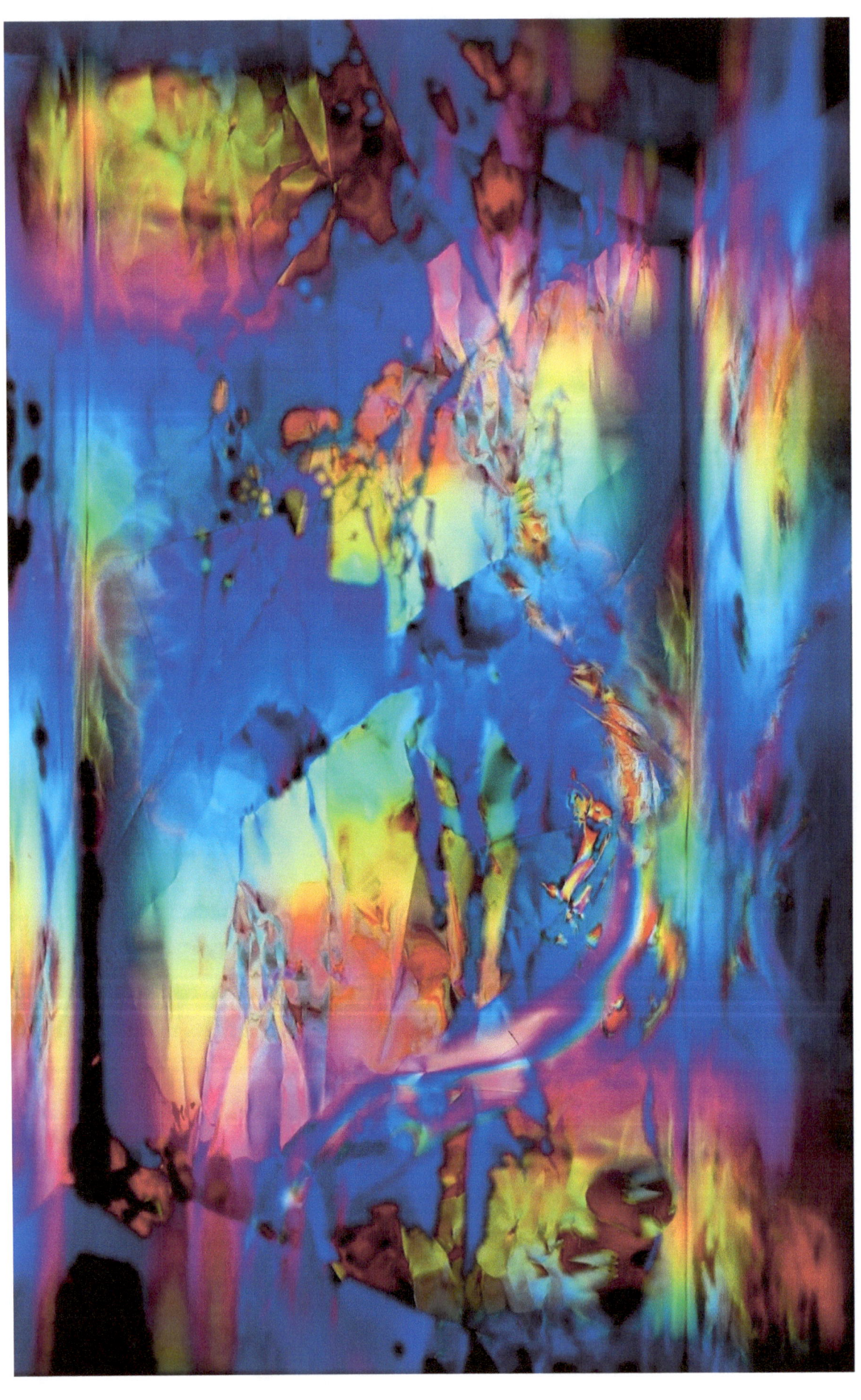

Higgs Boson

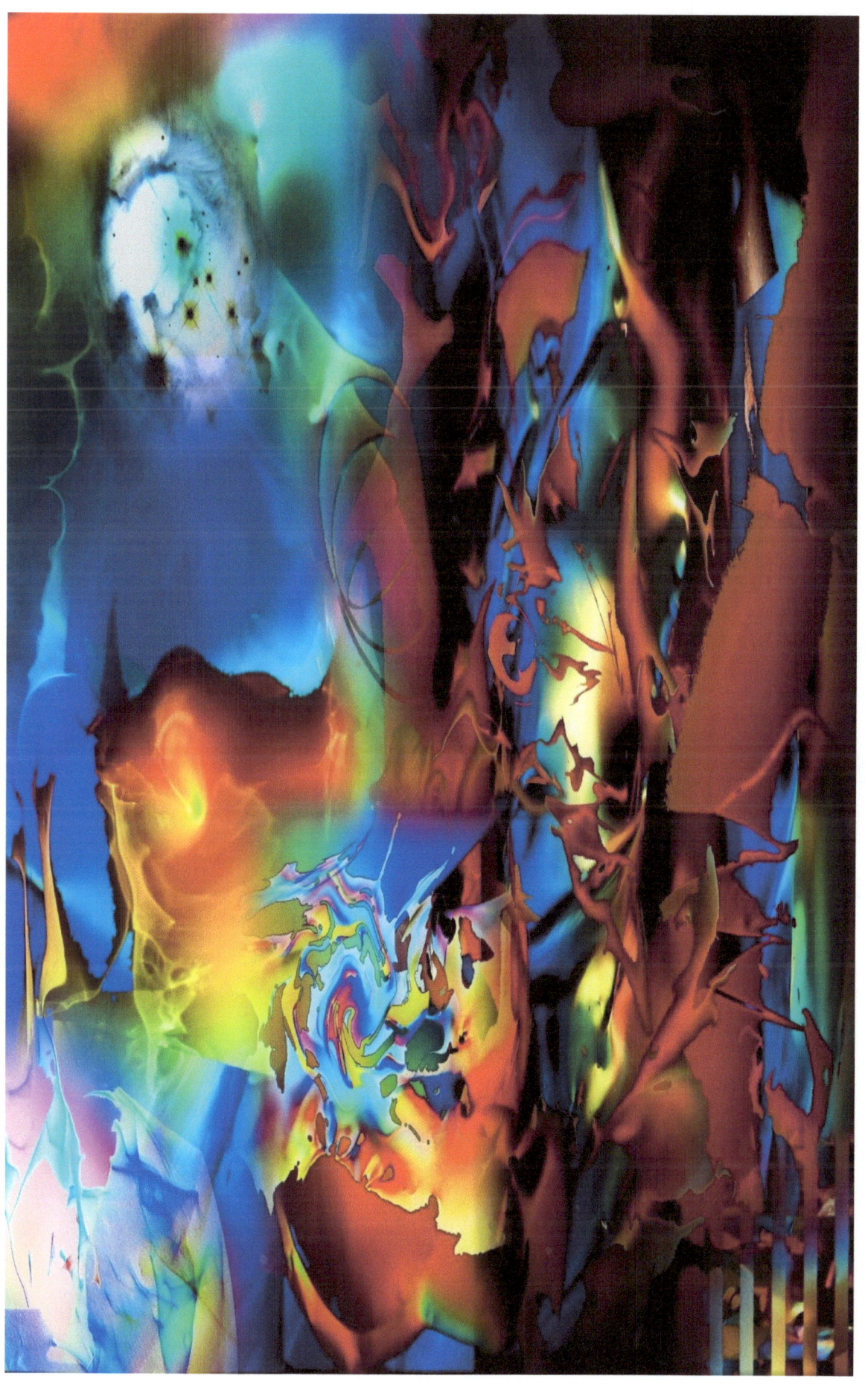

Ethereal Seizure

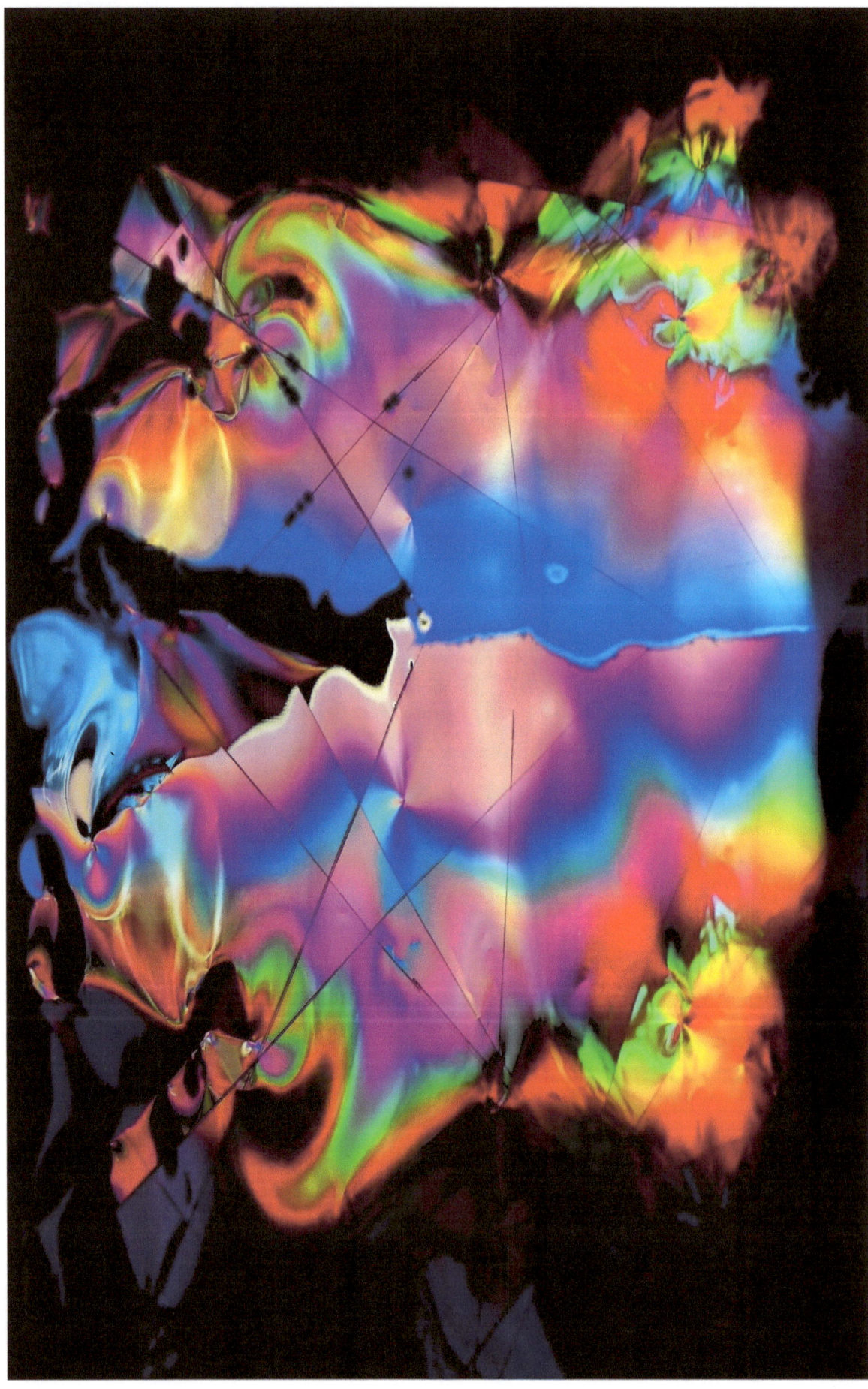

Hyperbolic Funk

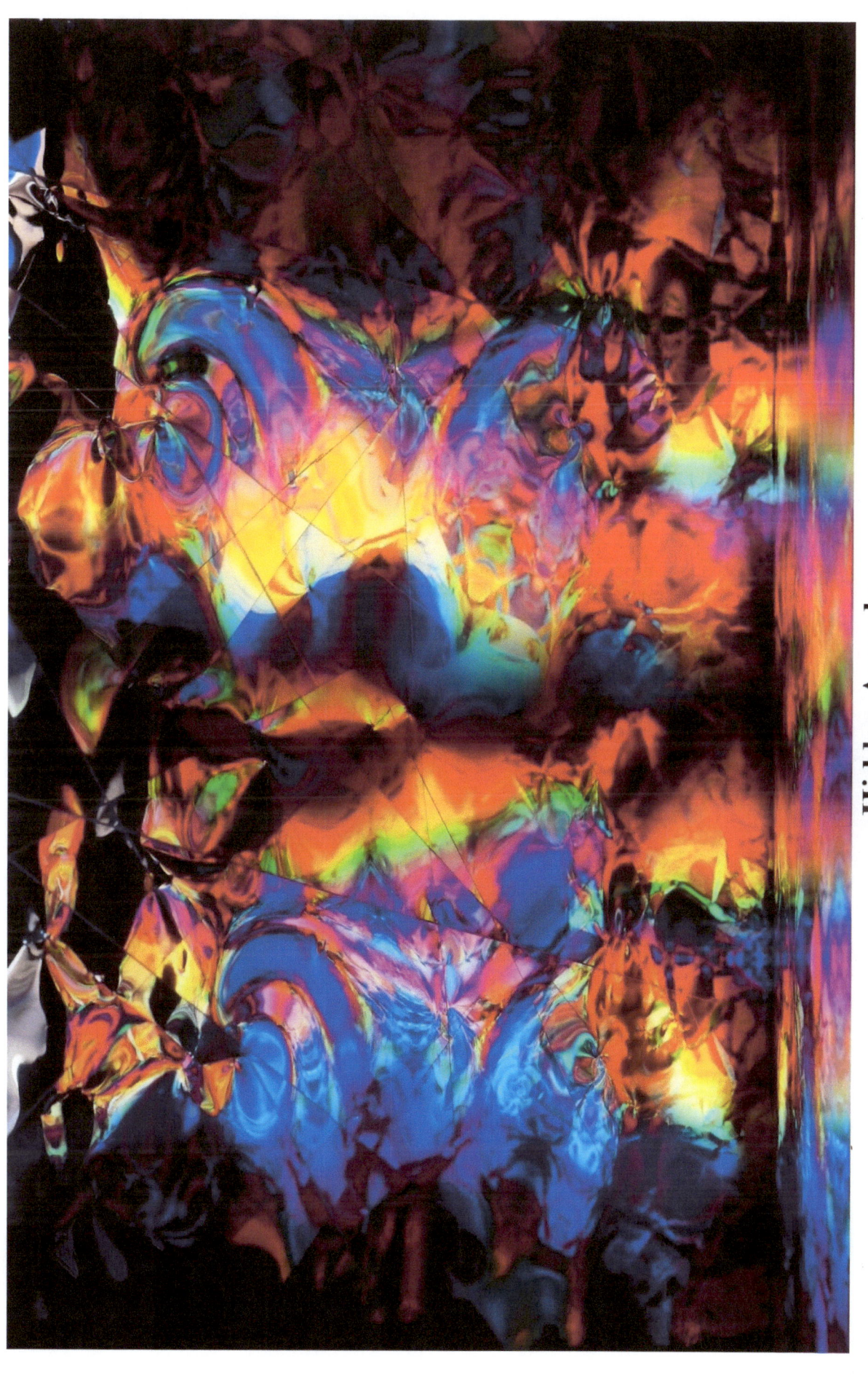

Hidden Agendas

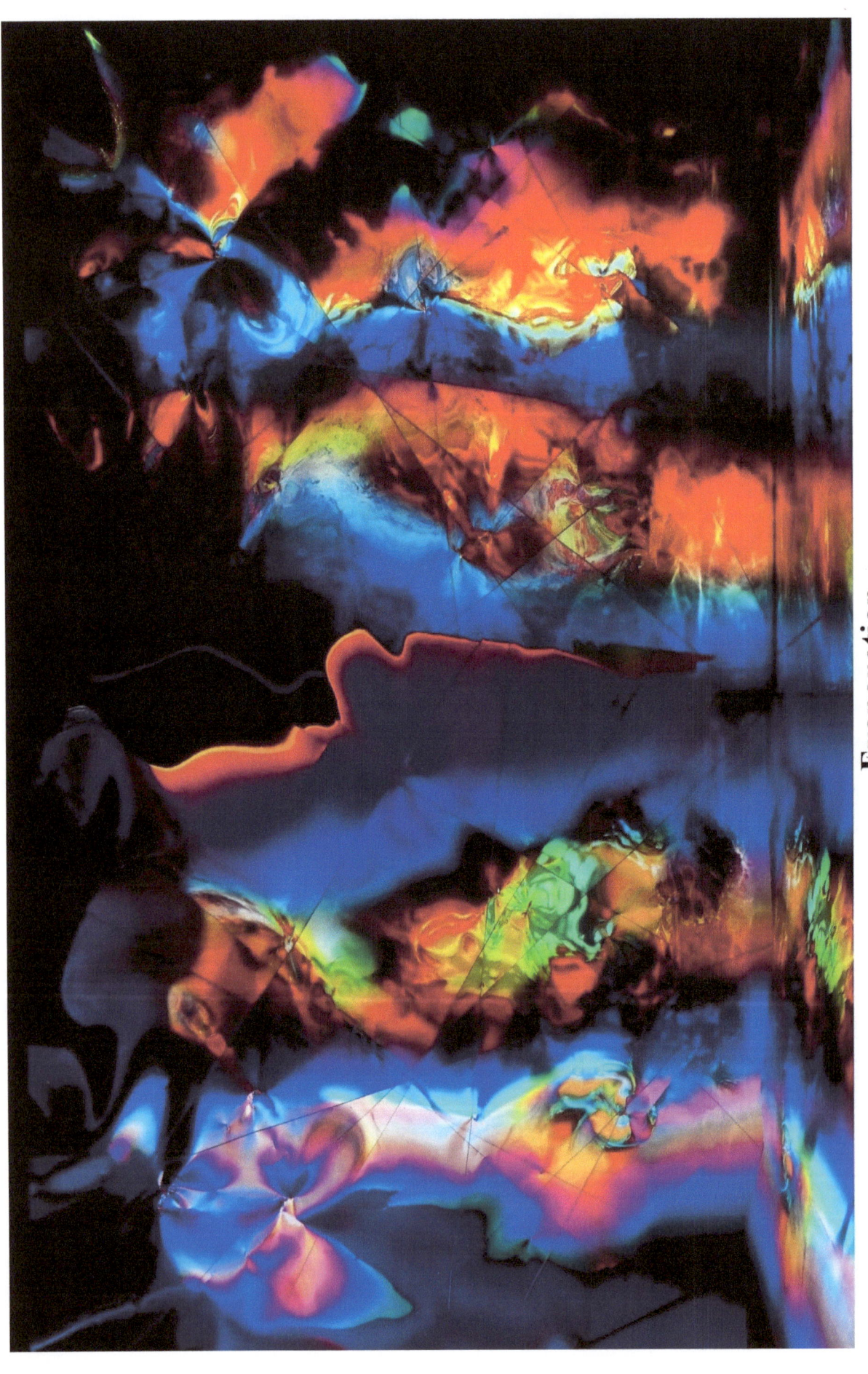

Evaporation

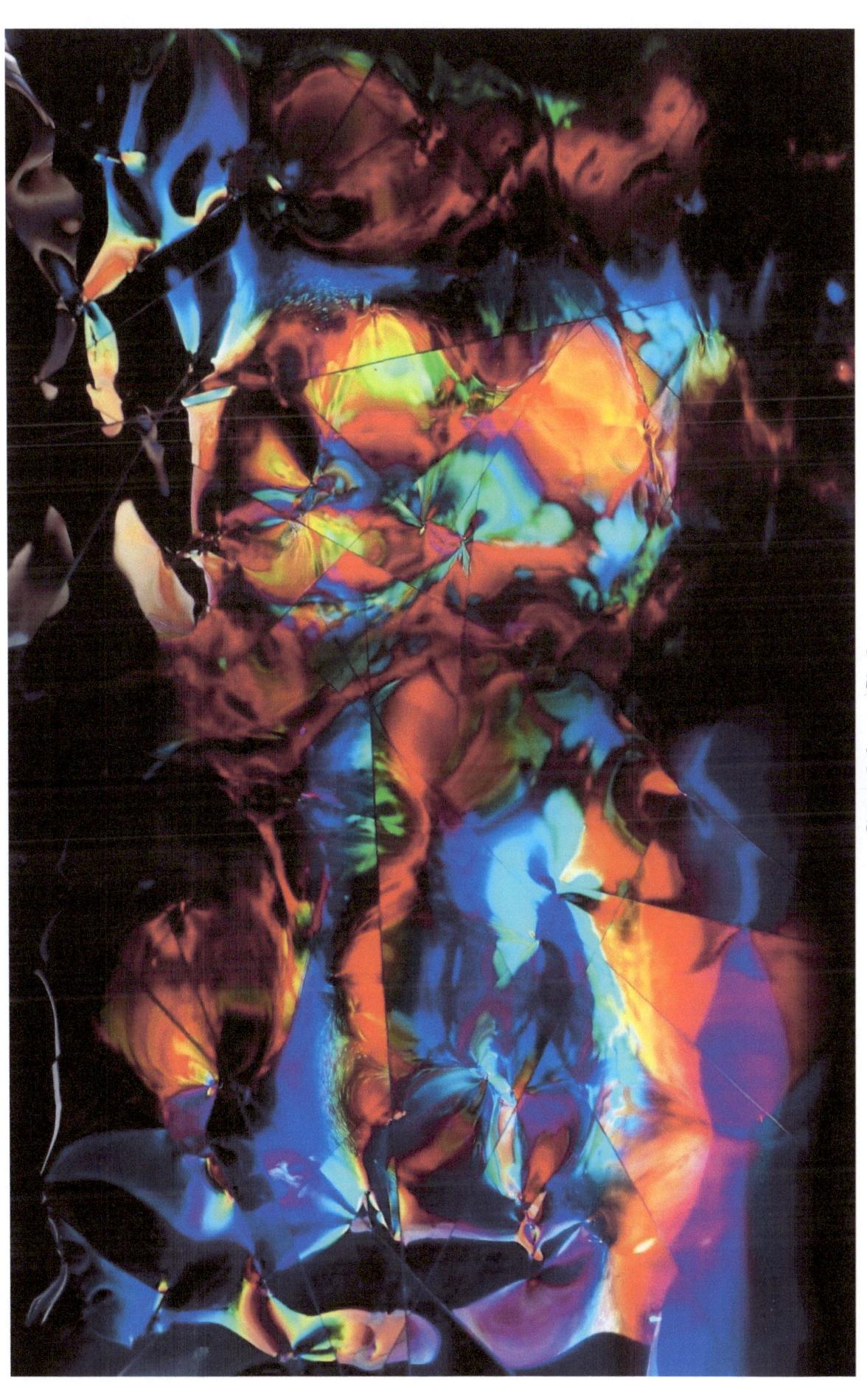

Seething Calm

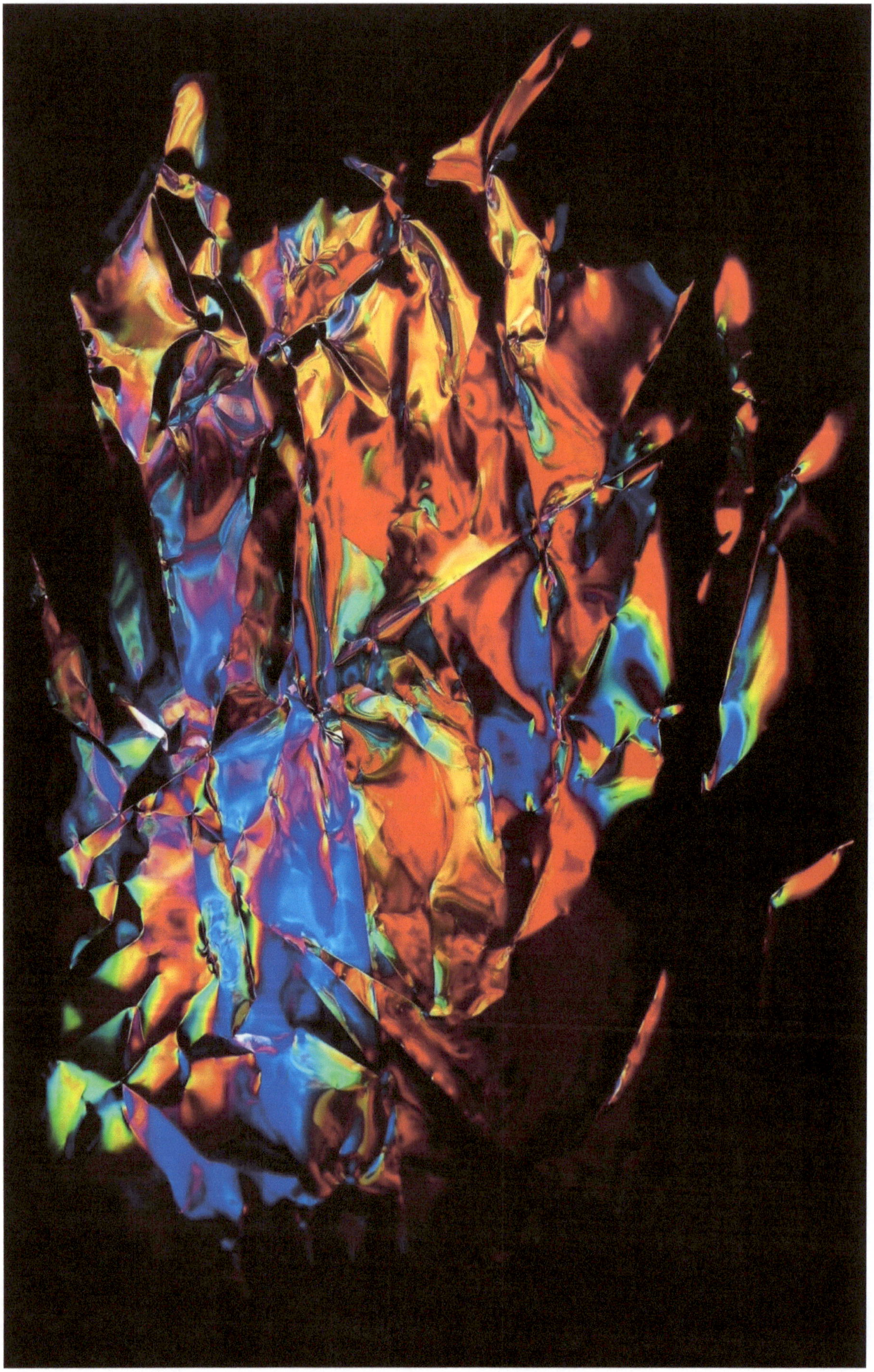

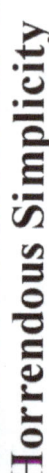

Horrendous Simplicity

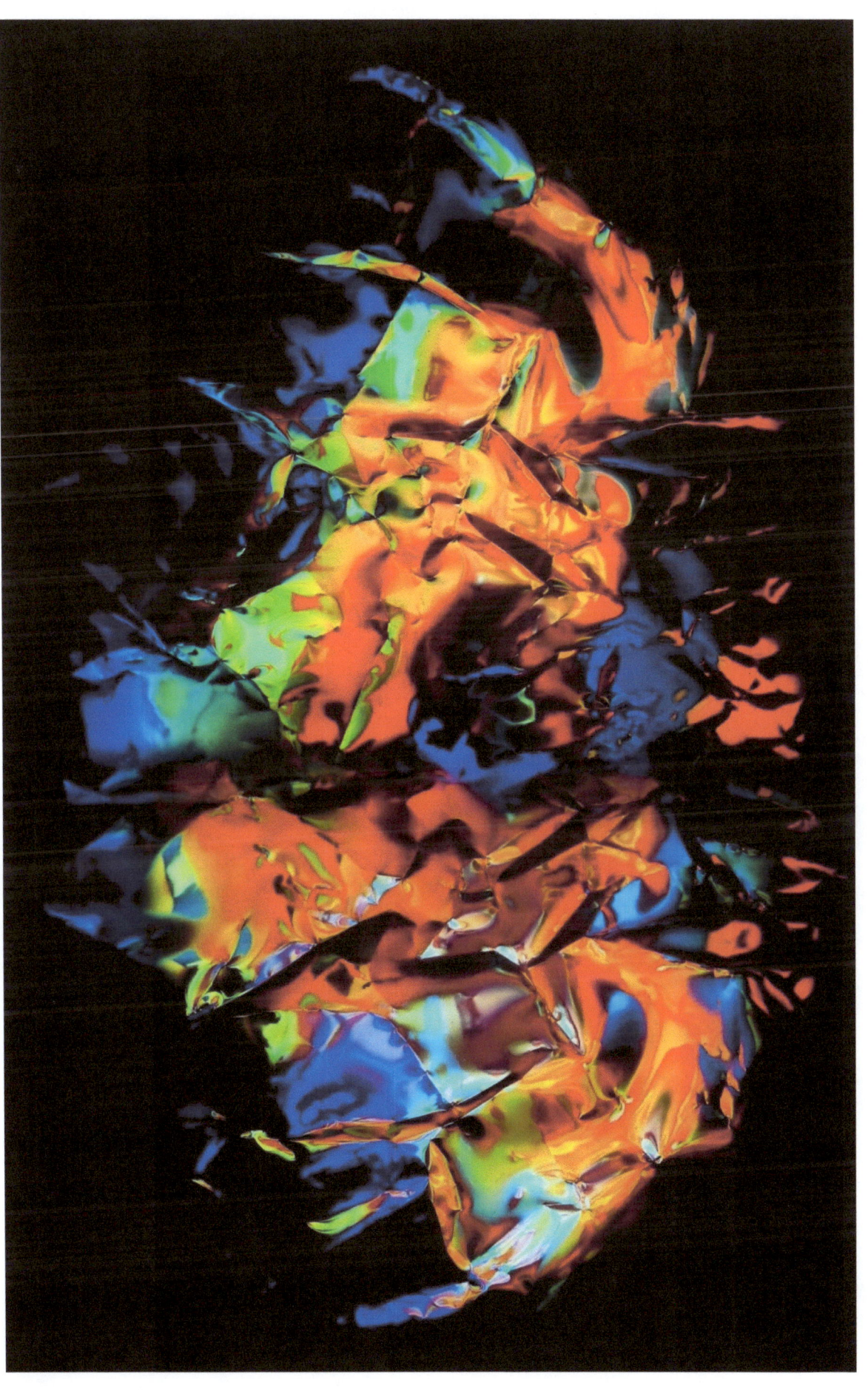

Reaching

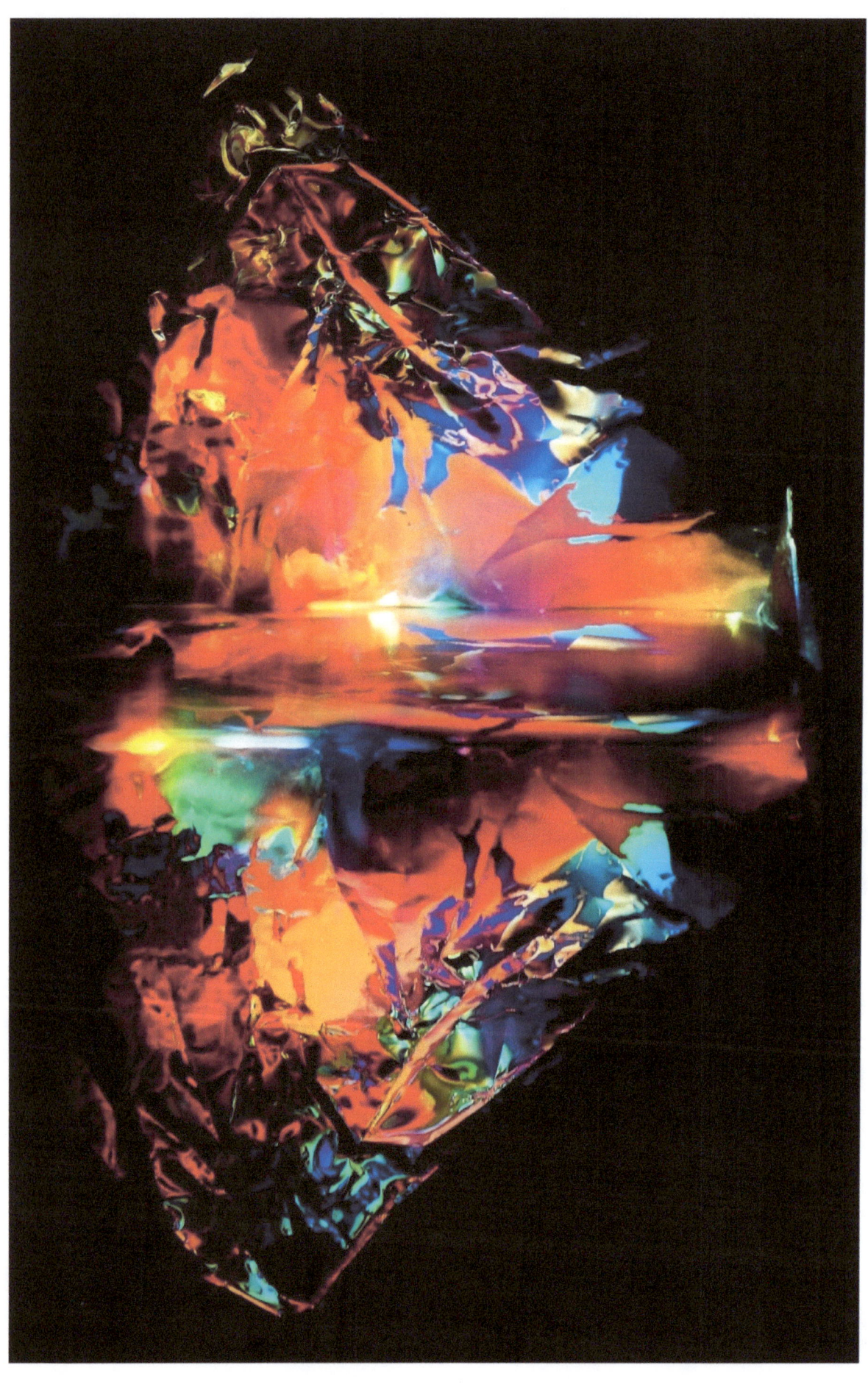

Light Heart

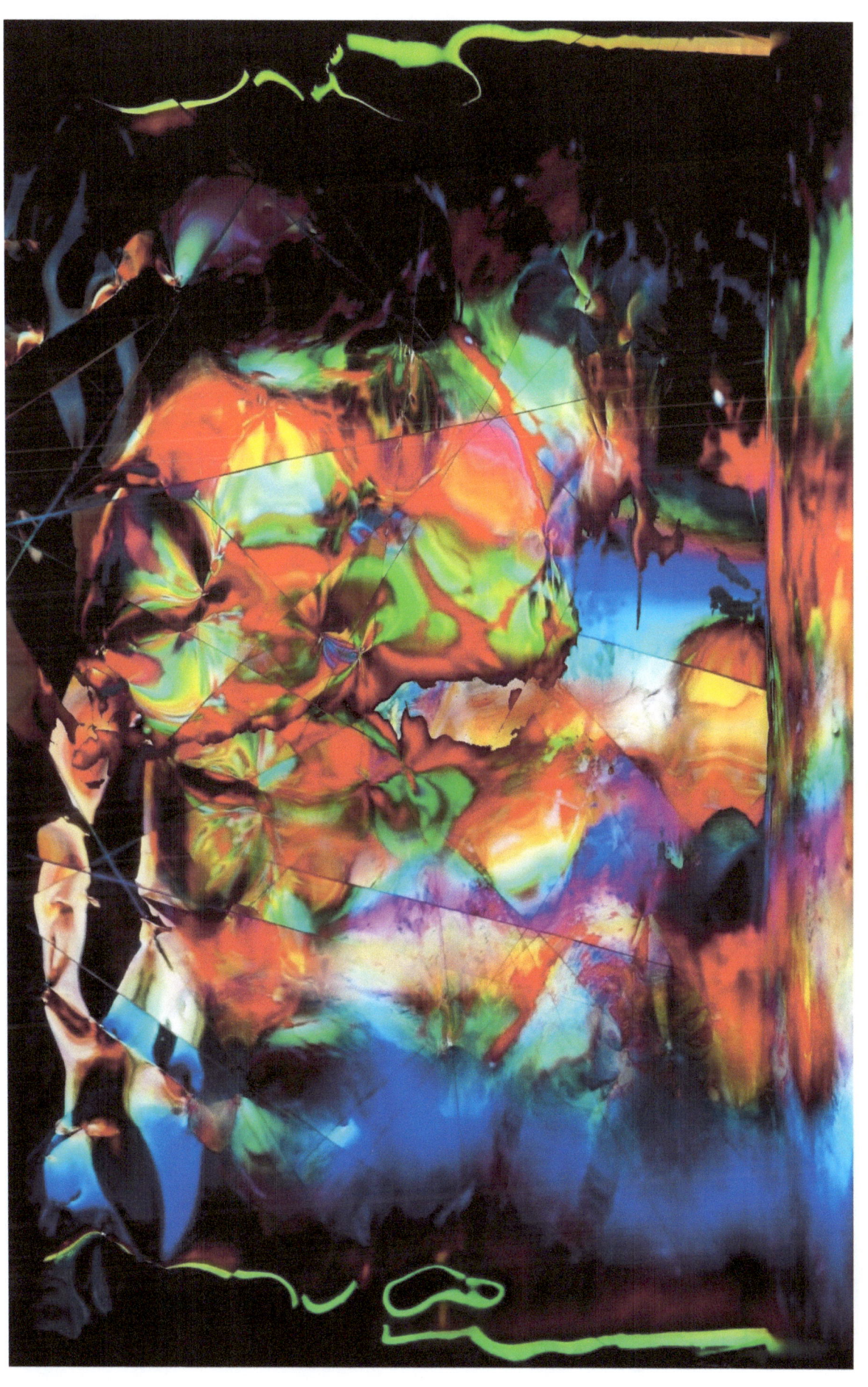

Saint Elmo's Fire

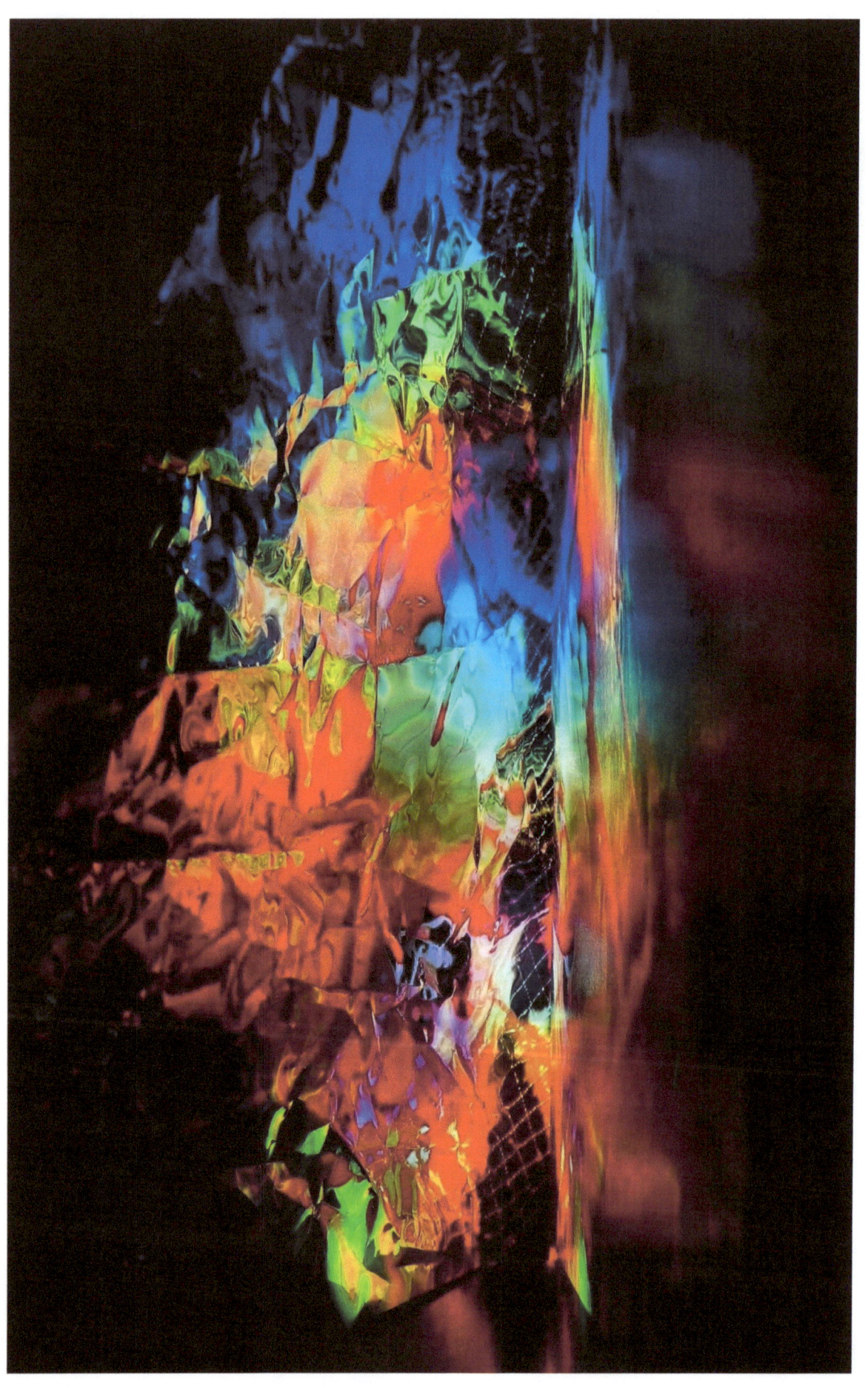

Net Effect

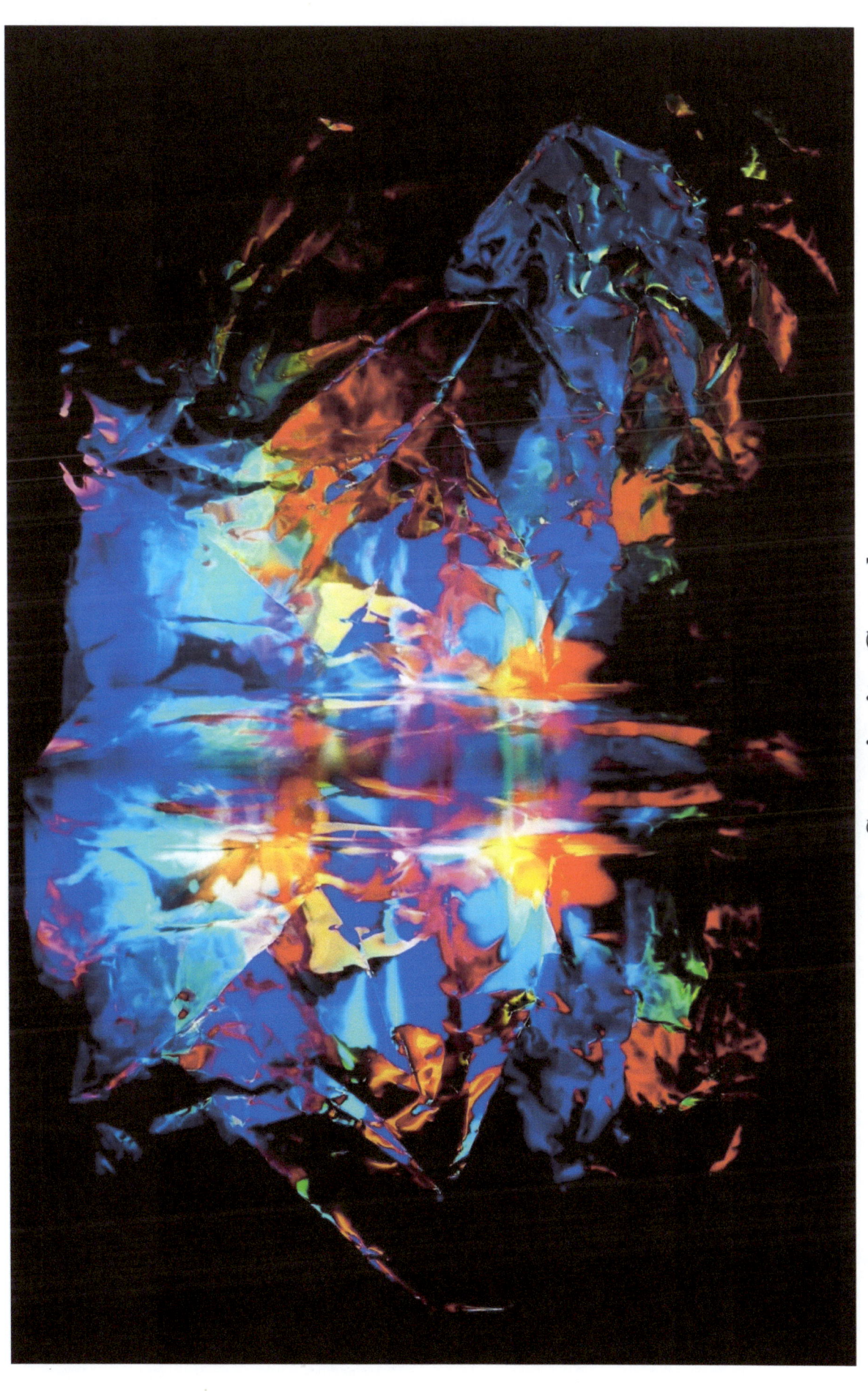

Superiority Complex

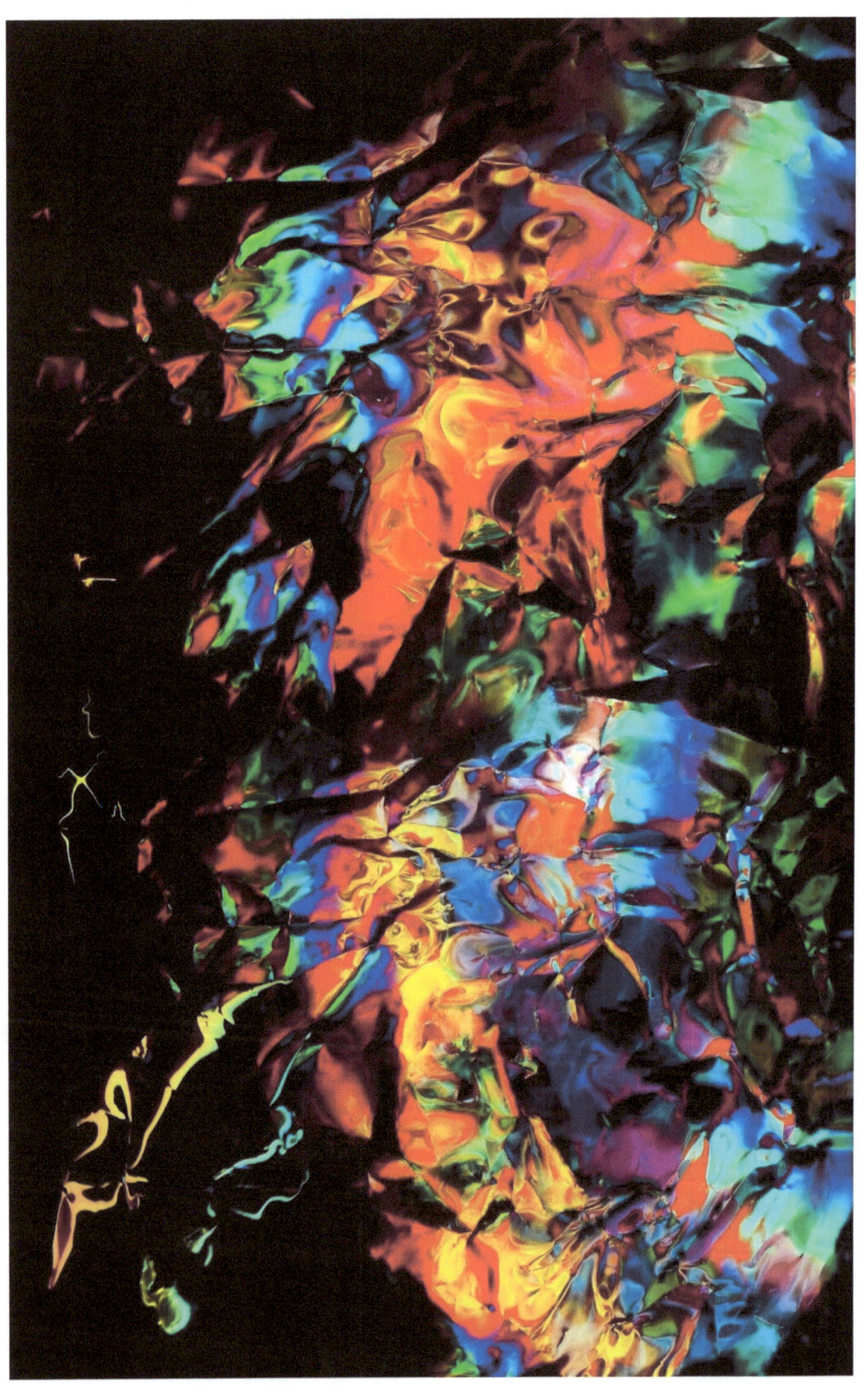

Momentary Laps

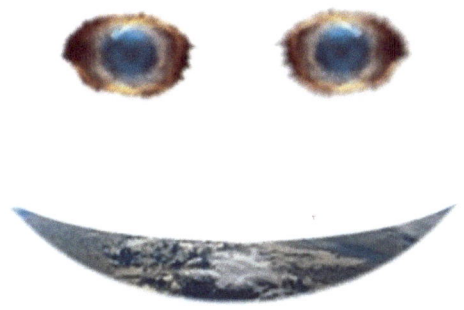

Thank You